making dolls

by h. witzig and g. e. kuhn

STERLING PUBLISHING CO., INC.   NEW YORK
Oak Tree Press Co., Ltd.
Distributed by WARD LOCK, Ltd., London & Sydney

OTHER CRAFTS BOOKS

Batik as a Hobby
Candle-Making
Cardboard Crafting
Carpentry for Children
Ceramics—and How to Decorate Them
Coloring Papers
Constructive Anatomy
Creating from Scrap
Creating with Beads
Creative Claywork
Creative Embroidery
Creative Enamelling & Jewelry-Making
Creative Leathercraft
Creative Paper Crafts in Color

How to Make Things Out of Paper
Knitting Without Needles
Make Your Own Mobiles
Make Your Own Musical Instruments
Metal and Wire Sculpture
Nail Sculpture
Original Creations with Papier Mâché
Papier Mâché—and How to Use It
Plastic Foam for Arts and Crafts
Potato Printing
Sculpture for Beginners
Stained Glass Crafting
Tin-Can Crafting
Weaving as a Hobby

Whittling and Wood Carving

Translated by Ingrid Froehlich

Second Printing, 1970

Copyright © 1969 by
Sterling Publishing Co., Inc.
419 Park Avenue South, New York 10016.
British edition published by Oak Tree Press Co., Ltd.
Distributed in Great Britain and the Commonwealth by
Ward Lock, Ltd., 116 Baker Street, London W1
The original edition was published in Switzerland under the title "Puppen" © 1965
by Eugen Rentsch Verlag, Erlenbach bei Zurich.
Manufactured in the United States of America
All rights reserved
Library of Congress Catalog Card No.: 69-19492
ISBN 0-8069-5134-6   UK 7061 2163 5
5135-4

Contents

Before You Begin

After you have read this book of instructions, you will be able to make a variety of dolls, ranging from simple ones of wire, twigs or stockings, to more complex ones of moulded material with thoroughly-jointed arms and legs.

Although most of our collection are dolls made by women, we also include examples which we hope will encourage men and boys to take up this hobby. Experience has taught us that men do as well as women in this craft. Although their creative efforts are at first usually directed more to the inventive use of the saw than to the use of needle, they soon realize that both skills are required. And women need not be frightened away by the mention of carpentry. Only a minimal use of the saw is required and the skill is easily acquired. In addition, there are so many methods of doll-making from which to choose, the use of the saw may be by-passed altogether.

The important point is that the constructive information furnished in this book will give you the confidence to develop your creativity. The illustrations of finished models should not be slavishly copied. Their essential meaning is to inspire you towards your own inventiveness in making dolls.

Illus. 1. This stuffed doll has a modelled head, movable joints and a nylon fibre wig.

Illus. 2. Even simple twig dolls can be jointed. See page 64 for instructions.

Dolls Made from Twigs

You can fashion a doll from the twig of a hazelnut or any conveniently available tree. All you need is a small saw and a pocketknife.

The twig should be approximately as thick as a thumb and about 8 inches in length. Later you will reduce the length to 4 inches with a horizontal cut. But for now the extra length will serve as a handle. Make two slight guide cuts on the upper end of the twig. Use the saw and make the first cut about 1 inch from the top of the twig. Make the second cut an equal distance from the first, as in Fig. 1.

Now use your knife to surround each

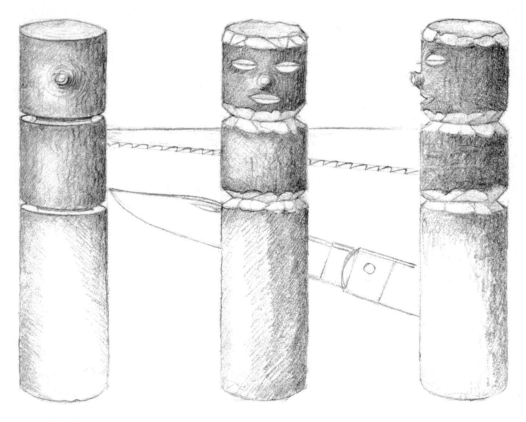

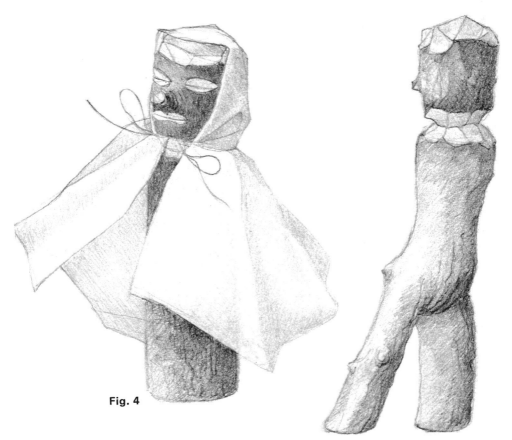

Fig. 4

Fig. 5

sawed cut with a circle of diagonal notches as shown in Fig. 2. Notch the edge on the upper part of the wood, too. This top section will be the doll's head.

This brings you to your last bit of hand-carving. First cut two notches facing each other to form the left eye. Do the same for the right eye. Then put a third pair of notches under them for the mouth (Fig. 2). In this way, using the stump of the small twig as a nose, you create the doll's face.

The finished work is shown in Fig. 4. The wooden man has been furnished with a decorative coat, made from red tissue paper.

Another variation of this doll can be made from forked branches (Fig. 5).

The twig doll is a very simple project and will be greatly appreciated by girls of from 4 to 7 years old. To them these dolls appear like magic guests from another world. Children will not tire of creating queens, princes and other fabulous beings from these dolls. Toys like these can stimulate the child's imaginative ability much more than if the doll had been bought in a store.

7

Dolls Made from Wooden Dowels

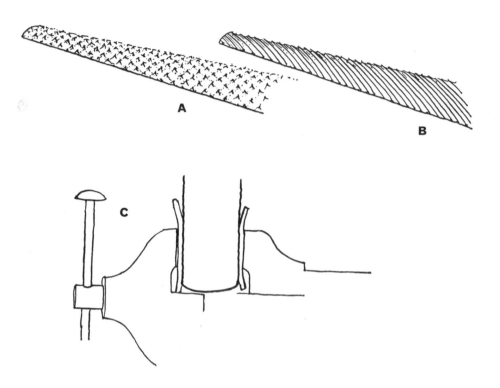

Standing dolls can be made from large, dried twigs, wooden dowels or an old broomstick. It is easier to use a rasp (A) and a file (B) instead of a knife on these rather hard woods. A small vise (C) can be used to hold the dowel while it is being worked on.

The dowel you use should be about five times longer than its width. (The line labelled *m* stands for the middle of the dowel in Fig. 1.) First draw a pencil line (*t*) to indicate the throat, about one-fifth of the way down from the top of the dowel. From there,

measure down about one-quarter the length of the dowel and draw a line (*w*) to indicate the waistline. Make saw cuts around these lines.

The cuts should not be made too deep; you can always cut deeper at a later time. Use a damp cloth or some cardboard while holding the dowel between the teeth of the vise. This is necessary to avoid slippage of the dowel and to keep it free from any damage.

Now, with your rasp, shape the form of

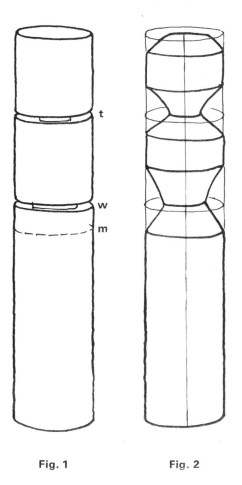

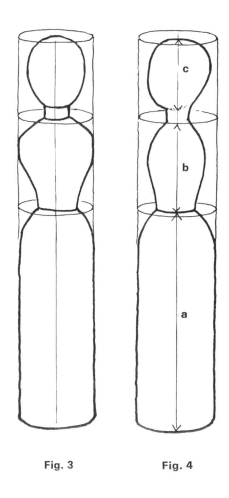

Fig. 1   Fig. 2   Fig. 3   Fig. 4

the waist and the throat (Fig. 2). Round the rough edges of the waist and chest smoothly with the file (Fig. 3). After you have shaped the throat as shown, the head will appear in a ball-like form.

As viewed from the side, the bottom piece (*a*) remains unchanged. But the chest and back (*b*) should be shaped as shown in Fig. 4. You also round off the head (*c*), on which you will paint facial features and hair.

Smooth the surface of the doll with sandpaper. Paint the face with moistened colored pencils. You can either paint on hair or paste woollen yarn on the head in such a way as to give the hair natural style. Making this doll is a suitable project for a 13-year-old child with adult supervision.

Wooden Dolls with Arms

These are dolls you can dress and even use to display in miniature various national costumes (Illus. 3, 4), which you can design from photographs. For this purpose the doll should not be too small, her arms should be movable, and she must have a good standing position. For this kind of doll you do not need to think about possible development of legs or feet. These forms are particularly suitable for costumes using long dresses or skirts.

Your material is a piece of an old shovel handle or wooden dowel, 8½ inches long and 1½ inches thick. The *upper half* should be subdivided into four equal parts, as shown in Fig. 1. The third of the four dividing lines (*a* in the diagram) indicates the waistline. On the second line (*b*) you pierce a ¼-inch diameter hole through the wood. To do this properly, clamp the dowel horizontally in a vise and use an electric or a hand drill. You will determine the final size of the head from the remainder of the top portion. Line *c* will indicate where the mouth is. Using that as a guide, indicate where the eyes are going to be.

Take the saw and, clamping the dowel vertically in the vise, remove the parts shown on the drawings in dark, hatched lines. First remove the parts shown in Fig. 1; then the parts shown in Fig. 3, which is the side view. From the top, the head and chest will appear square, as in Fig. 1a. Round the body-form (see the dark shading in Fig. 2 and the light shading in Fig. 3) with a rasp and a file as you did for the previous doll project.

Smooth the body with sandpaper. Next, pull a thick cord (which should be approximately five times the length of the head) through the hole you have drilled. Position the arms so they are of equal length. To indicate the wrist and hand, tie and fray the end of the cord as shown in Fig. 3. These flexible and revolving arms make it possible to pull a dress over the head of the doll. You can avoid misplacement of the cord and make it more stable by glueing it into position within the body of the doll.

Illus. 3. Dolls with cord arms and no feet are excellent for costuming.

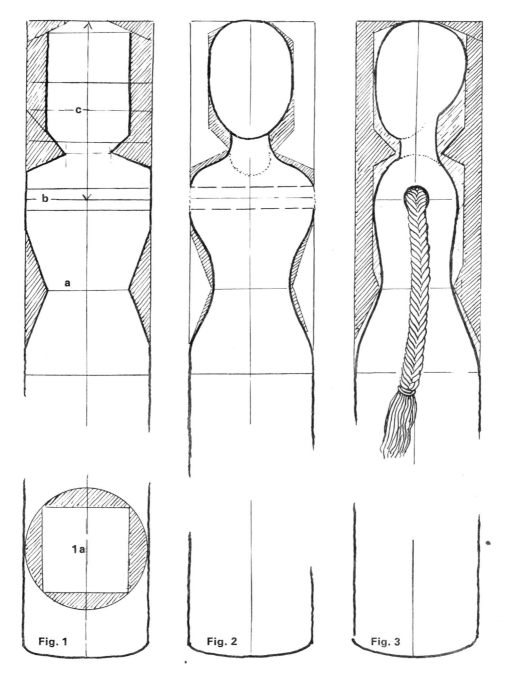

Fig. 1

1 a

a

b

c

Fig. 2

Fig. 3

11

Illus. 4. This dowel doll is dressed in a traditional folk costume.

Examples of Wooden Costume Dolls

Illus. 5.

Illus. 5: (*Left*) Dowel doll with yarn hair. (*Top right*) A doll with cord arms and yarn hair. She is about 5 inches high. (This is recommended for school children). (*Center*) A puppet made from a large twig according to instructions for dolls with arms. Note that below the hip region you should keep the original structure. The nose is formed from sawdust mass, which is discussed on page 32.

Sawdust is also used to shape the hands by covering the frayed cord. All parts, except the bark, are polished with sandpaper and painted over with two coats of water-based coloring. Use white, a little brown and a little red to establish skin color. The paint also helps to keep the cord rigid. (*Right*) This doll is also from a large twig. It is the work of a school child.

A Small Doll Made from a Glove

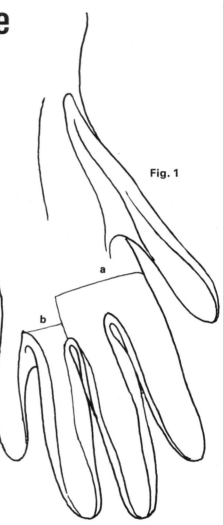

Fig. 1

Material for a doll can be obtained from any pair of old gloves that you have discarded. If the gloves are brown, you can make a Negro doll.

Using the *left* glove, cut off a section (*a*) including the forefinger and middle finger approximately ½ inch beyond the joint between the two fingers. The ring finger (*b*) which will be joined later by the ring finger of the right-hand glove is cut off also as shown in Fig. 1. Now you have perfect leg and arm covers (*a* and *b*). The covers for the body and the head are obtained from the left-over palm material. You cut this material into rectangles, two for the head and two larger ones for the body. They should be wide enough to allow for seams.

First pin together and sew the two rectangles forming the body. In the middle of the top edge, leave a hole for the throat; leave two slits open on the upper torso for the arms, and also leave the entire bottom unsewn (Fig. 2). Now reverse the sewn rectangle so it is right side out. After this is done, you stuff the body. The most suitable stuffing for such dolls is soft stockings.

Sew together three sides of the rectangles for the head, rounding out the two top corners as you sew. Turn the head right side out as you did with the body section and then stuff it completely, forming a rounded shape. The open end of the head is to be placed into the throat and sewn to the body.

Turn the raw edge of the body's throat opening under and use a hemming stitch to attach the head. In the same way you stuff and sew the arms and the legs to the body. Leave the ½-inch area at the top of the legs unstuffed so that you can insert it into the body opening and the doll will have the freedom to be placed in a walking or sitting position.

Fig. 3 shows a finished doll with black hair made from curled woollen yarn, an apron of silk yarn fringes, and shoes made from the fingertips of a leather glove. (By adding shoes, you conceal the difference in the length of the legs.) The shoes are stuffed with cotton. The bottoms are kept at a right angle to the legs with one or two stitches at the arch (c). (See Fig. 6, page 19.) The eyes, nose and mouth are embroidered. A white stitch gives the black eyes a realistic expression. For youngsters this is a robust baby doll.

Fig. 2

Fig. 3

b

a

c

A Handkerchief Doll

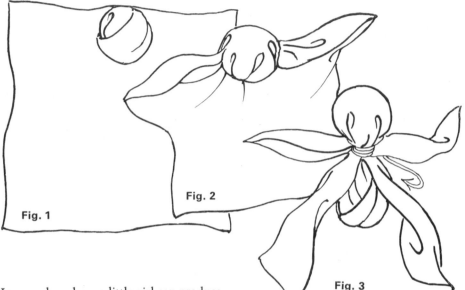

Fig. 1

Fig. 2

Fig. 3

Here we show how a little girl can produce a doll under the supervision of her mother or teacher. You need very few materials: an old handkerchief, a discarded pair of nylon stockings, and a ball of white woollen yarn.

Put the handkerchief in front of you. Now take one stocking, roll it together very tightly and pull the end over, making it into a ball. Place the ball on the top middle of the handkerchief (Fig. 1).

Turn the top of the handkerchief over, covering the ball with the material (Fig. 2). The ball will become the head of your doll.

Hold the folded handkerchief firmly in your left hand. With your other hand, take the ball of yarn and start winding it around and around exactly where the neck belongs (Fig. 3). Pull all the folds of the head towards you because the other side will become the face. Underneath the neck you will now have to place the body. Take the other stocking

and roll it up like the first one. Squeeze it into the shape of an egg and place it under the throat (Fig. 3).

Now wrap the handkerchief over the second ball. Next wind some yarn around this part of the handkerchief, covering it as far as the end of the body (Fig. 4). Continue winding the yarn back up around the body and then across each shoulder, thus forming the arms from the flaps left on top (Fig. 5). Remember to keep the ends free, as these will represent the hands. Repeat the winding process a third time down the body (Fig. 6).

Shape the legs by winding some yarn around the leg flaps. The feet are formed in the same manner you used to produce the hands, except that they are wound with yarn to make them sturdier. Finally wrap the

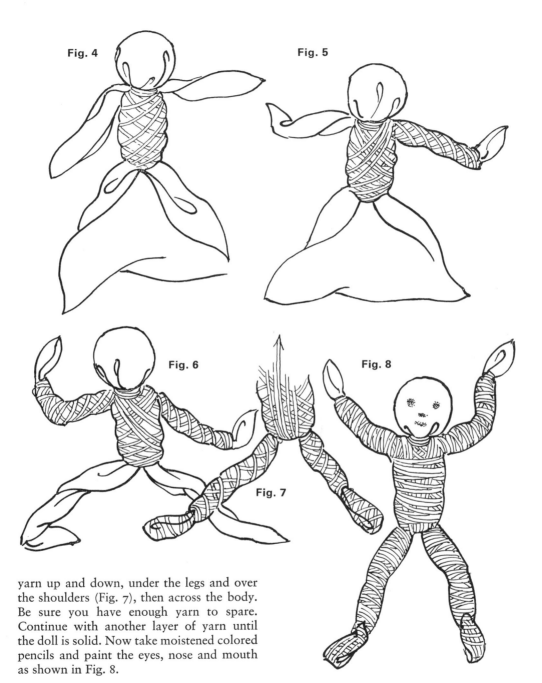

Fig. 4

Fig. 5

Fig. 6

Fig. 7

Fig. 8

yarn up and down, under the legs and over the shoulders (Fig. 7), then across the body. Be sure you have enough yarn to spare. Continue with another layer of yarn until the doll is solid. Now take moistened colored pencils and paint the eyes, nose and mouth as shown in Fig. 8.

A Doll Made from Stockings

Here is a procedure you can follow to make a doll from a discarded woman's stocking or from a man's nylon stretch sock. This is a good project for a 12-year-old girl.

First cut through the stocking, separating the foot from the leg (Fig. 1), with the intention of using the foot as a head and body cover. Then, stuff yarn or cotton or knitted remnants into the toe of the foot until you feel that there is a sufficient-sized head (Fig. 2). With some heavy thread (make sure it is the same color as the stocking) sew the stuffed head at the neck as shown in Fig. 3. Continue stuffing the rest of the body. Make the body one and one-half times the length of the head (a).

While holding the filled stocking in one hand, with the other hand, you pull back the heel flap, and pin, glue, and sew it strongly on to the back of the stuffed body (Fig. 4). This bottom flap is skilfully placed so that the doll is capable of an excellent sitting position.

Take the remainder of the material that you cut off when you first started this project. For each leg, you make a roll of appropriate thickness from part of the left-over stocking. Pull the inner edge of the material back over the rolled leg and glue it as shown in Fig. 5. Then pull the outer edge over and sew it over the rolled leg as shown in the same diagram.

At each open end of the tubes forming the legs, turn the material inward and sew it together with heavy thread (Fig. 6, a). One end of each leg is bent forward to make a foot.

Put a few stitches through the transverse fold (b) and the foot will remain in this position.

Now you attach the legs to the body. Place them in front of the body with the seam of each leg facing each other and sew them on to the body in a natural position (Fig. 7). They should not be sewn on too tightly or the doll will not be able to sit properly.

Two other rolls of stocking material are going to supply the arms. They are made like the legs (Illus. 5). For the hands you simply tie off a part of the arm in the area of the wrist. You may also add stitches to indicate fingers (Fig. 8). The arms are positioned so that the hands do not quite reach the middle of the doll's thigh. Any extra length can be cut off and discarded before you sew the tube ends (Fig. 8). Then the arms are sewn on to body in the same way as the legs were.

You may still not be satisfied. The most important fact is that the doll's head will have a tendency to fall over when she is sitting. Another thing which detracts from the doll is the stocking seam in the middle (unless you have used a seamless stocking). Therefore a piece of material without a seam (from a man's stretch sock, perhaps) is put over the head as shown in Fig. 9. Pull this material down to the throat; gather it together at the throat and sew it on to the head and body in a neat neckline (Fig. 10).

On page 21 (at the right) is an example of the finished doll. Her features are made from colored yarn. Her hair is made from white lamb's wool.

Fig. 1

Fig. 2

Fig. 3

a

Fig. 4

Fig. 5

Fig. 6

a

b

a

Fig. 7

Fig. 8

Fig. 9

Fig. 10

Illus. 6. Knitted doll at left made with stockinet stitch; one at right, garter stitch.

Illus. 7. At left is a handkerchief doll; at the right is a stocking doll.

Knitted Dolls

You may work more freely with knitted dolls. You don't have to follow the kind of exact instructions given for making previous dolls. For example you may design little childlike dolls. Each cover you are going to knit for the parts of the doll has a simple basic form. A knitted tube squeezed at the throat will make up the head and body. Arms and legs also are composed of tube-like forms.

First sketch the outline of the knitted doll on paper. Your sketch should have the same height as the doll you are going to make. With the help of the squares you are going to draw, you won't have any difficulty working with a given measurement.

After an outline of the desired doll is sketched, draw a vertical line (Fig. 1, a) through the middle of the body. On both the left-hand and right-hand sides of this line, you draw three other vertical lines equidistant from each other. Starting at the top of the doll, you draw the equidistant horizontal lines, and construct your graph pattern. In this way you may correct your sketch a little or work out remaining details.

Use a length of 12 inches for the final size of this doll. For the work, wool or cotton yarn is convenient. The best way is to knit a simple pattern such as a plain knit stitch, which should be tight so that the stuffing for the doll cannot be seen through the knitted pattern. You begin with the single head-and-body tube. Following your sketch carefully, you count the number of stitches needed for the width on the graph (b) and then multiply by three. If the tube on the graph measures 15 stitches, for instance, you will have to knit a width of 45 stitches in order to surround the whole body.

You sew up the top of the knitted tube; then stuff it loosely with pieces of old rags or towelling. Straighten the tube at the bottom and sew it into a rounded end. Wrap the throat with yarn to form the head of the doll and sew the yarn securely into place.

For big dolls of 14 to 22 inches, arms and legs are also knitted in tube form and stuffed. For very small dolls, flat knitted pieces can be substituted for tubes. Whether flat or tube-shaped, the limbs are sewn on to the body of the doll in natural positions. For a good sitting position of the doll, we recommend stuffing the legs loosely before sewing them on to the body.

The feet are made the way you would knit the toe part of socks. After stuffing they are bent forwards and kept in this position with a few stitches (Fig. 2). You can either knit the foot on at the end of the leg tube before stuffing, or you can knit the foot separately and attach it after stuffing.

Formed from the bottom part of the arm, hands are bound off at the fingertips and wrapped with yarn at the wrist (Fig. 3). Hands are stuffed more loosely than the arms. The hands of little dolls do not have to be stuffed at all. Facial features are embroidered on, and hair is made of yarn.

In the photograph on page 20, the doll at the left is made entirely of tubes, using the stockinet stitch. The doll at the right is knitted with the garter stitch, with hands and feet in the stockinet stitch.

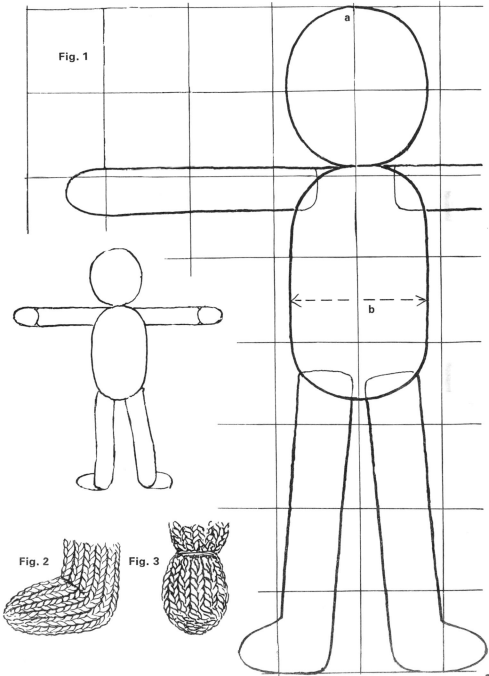

Fig. 1

a

b

Fig. 2   Fig. 3

23

A Tiny Figure for a Doll House

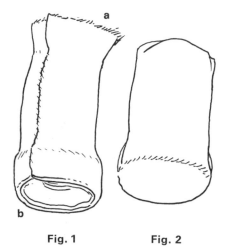

a

b

Fig. 1   **Fig. 2**

The figure should not be longer than 4¾ inches. It is made out of five separate pieces.

To begin the body for this doll, roll a piece of paper 1½ inches long into a tube that is about ¾ inch in diameter. Use glue to paste it together. Over the tube wrap a 2½-inch-wide cotton strip so that ½ an inch extends from either end of the paper tube (Fig. 1). Glue the material to the tube. The sitting area of the doll is determined by tucking in the bottom edges (*b*) of the cotton strip. The top edges (*a*) are also tucked in.

Now a piece of tricot material is used to cover the paper roll. The edges at top and bottom are pasted and sewn to form a life-like body (Fig. 2).

Next make the legs. The length of each leg and foot together is approximately 2 inches. Wrap and glue another piece of tricot material over a cardboard strip ⅛ inch wide and about 4 inches long (Fig. 3, *a*), forming a roll. Tie the ends of the roll with yarn to form feet and cut the strip in the middle to

form the two legs. These are then glued and sewn on to the front of the sitting level of the doll in a natural position. Bend the cardboard inside the tube at the point where it is tied, to give the feet a natural appearance. Carefully fold the open ends of the feet inward and sew them shut. (See finished doll, Fig. 7.)

The arms consist of a single length of ⅛-inch cardboard 4 inches long (Fig. 4). The strip is first covered with tricot material to make a roll in the same manner as the legs. After you have glued the edges of the tricot material along the full length of the arms, tie off the wrists with yarn as you did with the feet. Then attach the arms by sewing the entire roll to the top of the doll's torso as shown in Fig. 6. Then sew the hands in the same way as you did the feet.

The head is made from a little ball of cotton covered with yarn (Fig. 5). This again is wrapped with tricot material which is pulled together at the neck. With a few stitches, the head is then attached to the torso. Fringed linen material is used as a wig to cover the folds of the tricot material on the back of the head (Fig. 6). Or curled wool or Crimean lambskin may be used for the doll's hair. Facial features can be painted on with moistened colored pencils. However, they look much better if they are embroidered with colored thread. The finished doll is shown in Fig. 7.

As a variation to the procedure just described, you can eliminate the paper and the cardboard strips. You simply form the torso and roll the legs and arms from any convenient cloth; then cover the parts with tricot material. If made in this fashion, the doll can be crumbled and crushed without damage.

a

Fig. 3

Fig. 4

Fig. 5

Fig. 6

Fig. 7

Body Proportions

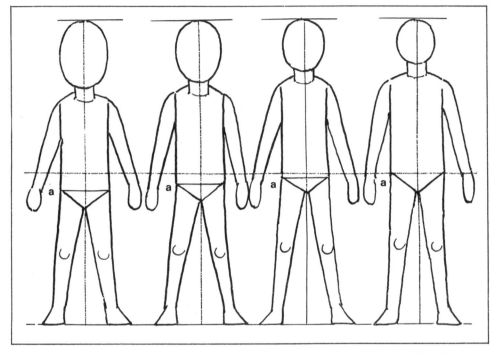

Basic considerations used in the shaping of a doll are the dimensions of the single body parts. At the top of the page, we show four outlines of human figures, all of the same size but in different age groups, progressing from a 2-year-old to an adult. When you compare the size of the head with the length of the body, you soon realize that the body proportions of the four figures are different from each other. In the illustration, you will notice that, from left to right, the heads are respectively four and one-half times, five times, six times, and eight times the length of their bodies.

Also the other parts of the body change;

for example, from left to right, the legs get longer in relation to the length of the body. In our illustration you can see how the line indicating the first child's waist is approaching the hip line (a) of the other figures, and finally both become a single horizontal line in the adult figure.

Note, too, that the arms, measured with respect to the length of the head, are becoming longer. Although the arms barely reach over the head in the case of a baby, older people can reach their ears when placing their arms across the head. Also, in studying head-body relationships you should realize that the width of the head as viewed

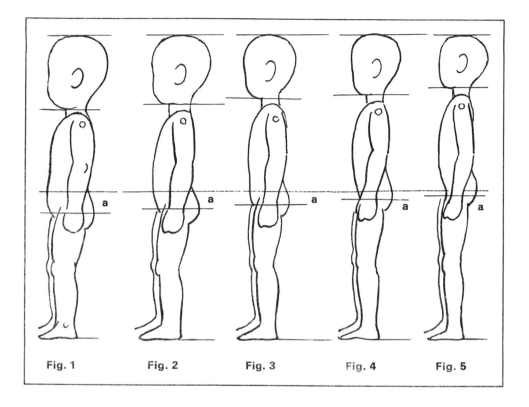

Fig. 1   Fig. 2   Fig. 3   Fig. 4   Fig. 5

from the side is approximately equal to the width of the body's profile as shown in the illustrations at the top of this page.

During your work you should refer to the drawings on page 26 and keep in mind the following résumé of the five steps in childhood:

Fig. 1: The total size equals four times the length of the head at 2 years old.

Fig. 2: The total size equals four and one-half times the length of the head at 3 years old.

Fig. 3: The total size equals five times the length of the head at 5 years old.

Fig. 4: The total size equals five and one-half times the length of the head at 6 to 7 years old.

Fig. 5: The total size equals six times the length of the head at 7 to 8 years old.

A further guide line is that the arms (including the hands) are approximately as long as the legs when the leg is measured from the hip joint to the sole of the foot. The knee should be located midway between the hip joint and the sole of the foot. The elbow should be located midway between the shoulder and wrist. For information about the body proportions of babies see page 90.

If a doll's head appears too large, it should not automatically be viewed as being out of proportion. See the left-hand model on page 62. If the photograph is examined closely you will observe that a child's head must be relatively large to be natural.

Dolls Made from Foam Rubber

You can leave this doll with a baby in its bed or in a bathtub. Foam rubber is very light and can be bought in different colors and thicknesses.

The diagrams on page 29 show how to make a very simple doll. Cut three pieces of foam rubber into blocks 1½ inches thick, 2½ inches long and 2 inches wide. Divide two of these blocks in half lengthwise, thus producing four separate pieces. These pieces will represent the arms and legs. The third whole block will form the body of the doll, while a fourth block can be cut in a 2-inch cube to form the doll's head. These six pieces of foam rubber (Fig. 1) are now trimmed and shaped with scissors into rounded, lifelike forms (Fig. 2). When forming the legs, include the feet. For exact measurements, follow the principles of proportion given in the preceding chapter.

To unite these pieces, strings are pulled through the body, as shown in Fig. 1, with the use of a thick needle. The knotted ends of the strings will leave depressions, which you cover with small pieces of foam rubber (Fig. 1, a). Use glue to paste them on. Watertight glue will seal and fasten these knots into place. The hair and nose are also pasted rubber pieces (Fig. 3a). Use pieces of cloth to form the eyes and the mouth (Fig. 3).

You can also make a foam rubber doll that can sit. The legs and lower torso are cut at angles that meet, as shown in Fig. 4 on page 30. This forms a joint enabling the legs to be twisted towards you. Later chapters, beginning on page 58, deal with jointed dolls. But for now all you have to do is follow the diagram. From the drawing you can see how the legs and body are cut, and how the legs and arms are connected loosely to the body by strings. Also note that the leg is cut with a foot projecting at the bottom.

For eyes you can use beads or yarn. Set facial features made from beads or yarn into position with knots by pulling the string or yarn across through the head (Fig. 5). In this way, you can create eye sockets as well as dimples, obtaining a somewhat childlike expression for the face.

Fig. 6 on page 30 shows a foam rubber doll with wrapped body parts, viewed from the back. The body and head together are covered with one piece of cloth. One edge of the cloth is folded inward to form a flap (a) which is sewn overlapping the other edge to form a seam (b). The cloth is simply tied at the throat to separate the head and body.

At the top of the head, the cloth is pulled together and sewn. Arms and legs are made of rolled foam (c) and are wrapped and sewn in the same way. Fingers and toes are shown by stitches; wrists and ankles by tying with yarn or string. The arms and legs are then sewn on to the body of the doll in natural positions.

The photograph on page 31 shows a foam rubber, leg-jointed doll seated on the left side. The hair is made from dark-colored foam rubber. The eyes are glass beads. The nose is pasted on. The doll is about 8 inches high. The doll on the right side has eyes and a mouth made from silk yarn. Arms and legs are sewn loosely on to the body. The height of the doll is about 9 inches.

Fig. 1

Fig. 3a

Fig. 3

a

a

Fig. 2

29

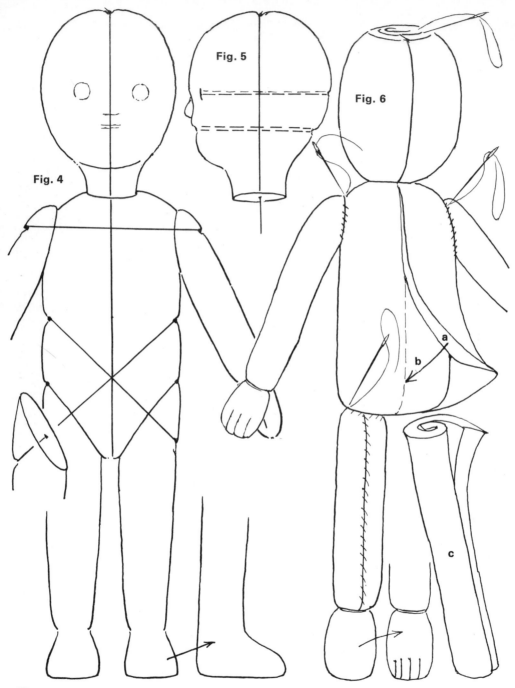

Fig. 4

Fig. 5

Fig. 6

a

b

c

30

Illus. 8. Seated doll is jointed by threads; standing doll has limbs sewn on.

Modelling Material

For your next dolls you are going to use material that can be modelled with your hands. This material should fulfill certain requirements.

You should be able to knead it easily between your fingers. After you have shaped the desired form, the material should become hard, stable and, if possible, unbreakable. It should not be heavy. Once it is hard, you should be able to work on it further. You should be able to saw, file, drill, smooth, grind, paste, and paint the substance. Also, you should be able to produce it by yourself in an easy and inexpensive way. Here we describe two such substances. The first is a very simple recipe using sawdust, cellulose glue and water. Sawdust is a material you can usually get very easily at timber-yards. Glues are available in powder or crystal form from stores that sell art materials or wallpaper supplies.

To prepare your modelling material, place the amount of sawdust you are going to use in a bowl and sift out the coarse material. Sprinkle binding glue into another bowl filled with a little water and mix the powder until it looks thick and jelly-like. Add this paste to the sawdust and mix both together very well until you can take out the mass from the bowl and knead it with your hands. If the mixture sticks to your fingers, it needs a little more sawdust. Once this material has been mixed it has to be used immediately. This is not true of our alternative material, papier mâché mash. One of the advantages of working with mash is the fact that it can be made in advance and kept. Mash improves in texture and consistency with ageing.

Whichever material you use, you model it with a palette knife, a small, sharp knife, or wooden sculptor's tools. How to proceed will be explained in the following chapters.

To make the mash, tear newspaper into narrow strips $\frac{1}{4}$ to $\frac{1}{2}$ inches wide. Tear the paper lengthwise. Gather the strips together in your hand. Next tear the strips crosswise into pieces about 1 to 1$\frac{1}{2}$ inches long. Fill a bucket or another large container with the dry, torn pieces of newspaper. Fill a large enamel bucket with water, which you bring to the boil. Into the boiling water, sprinkle the pieces of newspaper as if you were cooking noodles. Stir the pieces of paper to separate them well.

Cook the paper until the fibres are broken down and the paper has disintegrated. Add water from time to time if necessary to keep the bucket full. Add $\frac{1}{2}$ teaspoon of oil of wintergreen. This keeps the mash smelling sweet and prevents the growth of moulds and fungi.

Using a wire whisk or an egg beater, beat until the mixture is smooth. Any small pieces that happen to escape the beating process may be left in the mash.

Drain the mash in a wire strainer or a collander until there is no more water from the bucket left standing in the mixture. The mash will still be moist and will still contain much water.

To each gallon of mash that you have made add 4 measuring cups of flour. Mix well.

Now place the bucket back on the stove with an asbestos mat under the bucket. Cook at the lowest heat. Remember that flour scorches easily. Cover the bucket for the first hour until the mash has heated throughout. Remove the cover from the bucket and continue cooking (adding no water) until the mash is stiff enough to stand in piles by itself.

Dump the mash out upon about a dozen thicknesses of newspaper to cool. The mash may be used as soon as it is cool enough to handle or it may be stored in the refrigerator. In the winter, it is probably a good idea to let it reach room temperature before trying to work with it.

The heat of an oven, in the case of mash, or of the sun or central heating unit, in the case of sawdust, will be necessary for drying and hardening your finished models. (Mash can be worked in layers of up to 1 inch before it must be dried. Oven temperature should be 250 degrees F. Layers of sawdust material should be dried when they are about ¼ inch thick.) Since water is being evaporated from your finished models, they will shrink a bit (about one-tenth of their original size in the case of sawdust material), but they can be built up again without any difficulties. Alternatively, the moist models can be made larger than the desired final size to allow for this anticipated shrinkage.

When working on dried models, a file and sandpaper can be used. The finished models can be painted as desired. They should, however, have a watertight covering such as lacquer or wax. You will be using your modelling material for most of the projects in the following chapters, so study carefully the directions on its preparation.

Modelled Dolls with a Wire Frame

This chapter is devoted to creating little standing dolls with pliable joints made from wire. The wire frame (Fig. 1, page 35) is constructed for all body parts. The proportions are indicated by transverse lines on each wire and by the positioning of the framework. The unit for measurement is the head with its length of 1 inch. Two wires have a length of six units (6 inches) each with an additional one-half unit ($\frac{1}{2}$ inch) for the foot. The third wire connecting the head and body is two units long (2 inches). A cardboard pattern (Fig. 2) is shaped and cut out to be used as a basic form for the body. This, as well as the arms, legs, and head will be covered with your modelling material.

If you want the material to adhere firmly you must first coat the wire frames with glue and then wrap them with yarn. (See Fig. 6.) As you can see from Fig. 7, only part of the wire will be modelled, the rest being pinned and glued to the cardboard body. For a good standing position, a cardboard form should be pasted under the wire piece which will form the foot (Fig. 6).

First model the legs as shown in Fig. 6a and the arms as shown in Fig. 6b. Each arm and leg has to be modelled like a spindle. Apply the modelling material to the yarn-covered wire and shape the hands and feet as well as the legs and arms.

Using the modelling material, roll the head like a ball and then stick it on to the end of the third wire (Fig. 4).

Cover one side of the cardboard form with your modelling material to form the back of the puppet (Fig. 5). Wait until it is dry, then glue and pin the wire to the front of the card-board (Fig. 7) and apply material to form the front of the doll's body. When the material is dry, remove the pins and fill in the holes with more modelling material.

You will notice that the joints, such as at the knee, have been left exposed. This is so you can bend the wire into the positions you desire. Fig. 3 shows the finished doll. However, in that illustration the wires are set into the doll horizontally instead of vertically, with each length of the unmodelled wire (across the shoulders and between the legs) being equal to the length of the head. The steps are the same, and you can use either method of arranging the wires.

As a variation you can make these dolls with pipe cleaners. Pipe cleaners are sold in bunches. They are usually about 6 inches long. Because of their brush-like cotton covers, these pliable wires, which are quite strong, can easily be used for making small dolls.

You can either use the pipe cleaners by fixing them to the cardboard body as before or by bending them as shown in Fig. 8, page 36, and winding a third pipe cleaner around the two bent ones in a spiral-like form as shown in Fig. 9. However, in neither case are the arms and legs covered with modelling material. The head is formed in the same fashion as for the wire-frame doll.

Fig. 10 and 11 show how to combine model material with the pipe cleaners. Parts labelled *a* are covered with the material while parts labelled *b* are left exposed. Fig. 12 shows how the hands should be modelled at the ends of your pipe cleaners. A small coin (Fig. 13, *a*) modelled into the material will give a better

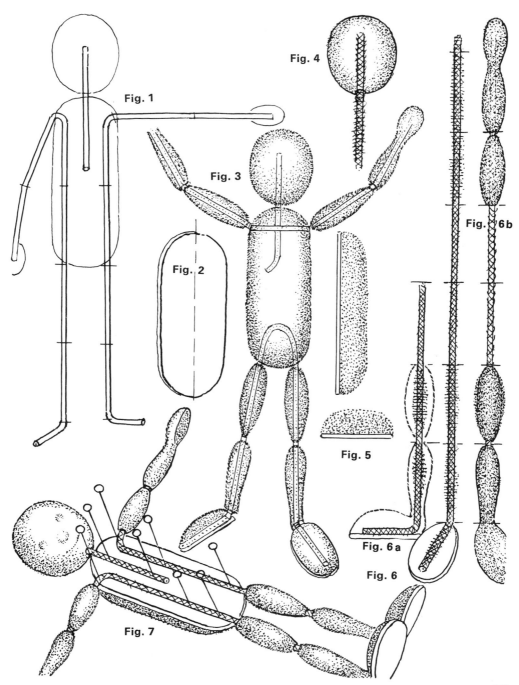

Fig. 1

Fig. 2

Fig. 3

Fig. 4

Fig. 5

Fig. 6

Fig. 6 a

Fig. 6 b

Fig. 7

35

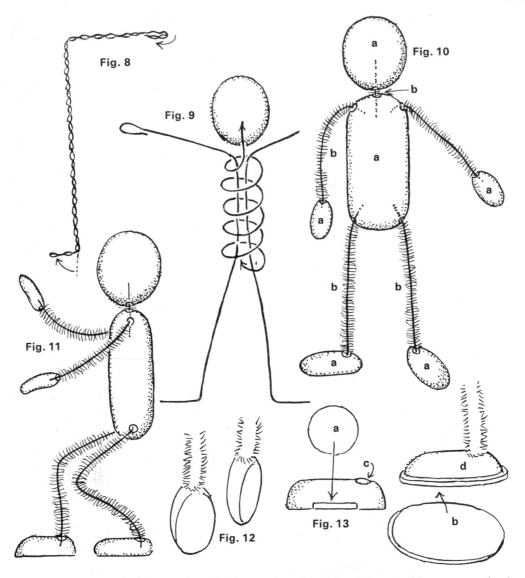

Fig. 8

Fig. 9

Fig. 10

Fig. 11

Fig. 12

Fig. 13

standing position for the feet. When the feet are dry, a cardboard form (Fig. 13, *b*) glued under each foot will give a good sole. The hands and feet are formed by rolling the material between your fingers and then flattening the shapes. With a nail, you punch holes into the feet (Fig. 13, *c*). After the feet dry, the ends of the pipe cleaners are glued into them (Fig. 13, *d*).

Examples of various wire-joint dolls are shown on page 37. The hair is also made from model material, which has been shaped with a pointed knife.

Illus. 9. Pipe-cleaner dolls in foreground have modelled bodies and heads. Wire-frame dolls in background have modelled limbs as well.

Doll Heads

Here we are concerned with creativity in making a doll's head, no matter what material you are working with. You may progress from a simple to a more sophisticated form, but you should always preserve a lively expression in the doll's face. The charm of a childlike expression should always be kept.

The basic form of the head is a more or less oval shape, which is placed on a well-rounded throat (Fig. 1, this page). This head form is most suitable if it is about the size of an egg, but it may also be larger if desired. It is important that the head be smooth and simply shaped. You have to consider that if the doll has a simple body it also acquires a simply-shaped head. Simplicity will be particularly appreciated by children.

If you compare the shape of the head in Fig. 2 with that in Fig. 3, you will notice, in the latter illustration, a large notch or flattened groove going from the back of the head to the neck. This shape more closely resembles the form of the human head, which can be divided into two parts (Fig. 4): a skull-capsule (*a*) and the face (*b*). The tube making up the neck and throat is positioned at the unfilled space.

Now your attention to the natural details of the neck, throat and head becomes important. As on your own facial structure, the change from the throat to the face must be smooth. These transitions are shown in Fig. 5 and 6. There should not be any sharp or rough edges. The back of the head is wide and becomes a very softly modelled arch (*a*). The edge of the jawbone projects only slightly from the neck tubing (*b*). The angle

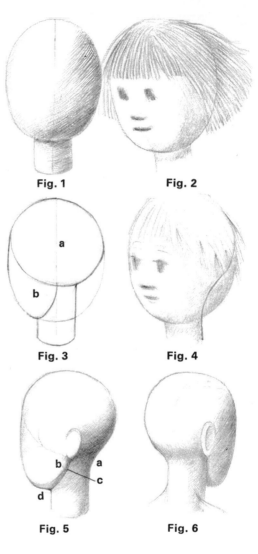

Fig. 1　　　　Fig. 2

Fig. 3　　　　Fig. 4

Fig. 5　　　　Fig. 6

of the jawbone shows a pronounced line (*c*) proceeding toward a horizontal line at the chin (*d*).

After you have studied the basic form, your next job is to supply this head with facial details. Here you have the opportunity to point out the characteristics of a child's head in your own creative manner.

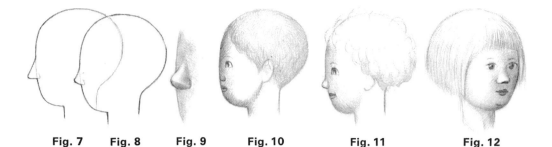

Fig. 7   **Fig. 8**   **Fig. 9**   **Fig. 10**   **Fig. 11**   **Fig. 12**

The nose is the feature which gets the most attention on a face, particularly in profile. Fig. 7, above, presents a nose that would belong to an older person. In Fig. 8 you see a child's nose. The form of the nose is most important for characterizing childlike aspects of a doll's head.

You are free to create a nose in any variation, but keep in mind that it should have a short nasal bone. You can make it wide, but not too large. The tip of the nose should fall in an oblique position (Fig. 9).

In Fig. 10, the nose is indicated with colored pencil. While the other painted facial parts appear natural to you, the nose seems to be unreal. In Fig. 11, the nose, indicated by a slanted little peg belongs to the face. Fig. 12 shows a doll's head with a finished nose. Eyes, mouth, eyebrows and chin are indicated by colored pencils. The doll has a wig made from artificial hair.

Divide the head as seen from the front into quarters (Fig. 13). The nose is placed at the second lowest quarter of the head. The head of a child is generally recognized by the relative height of the forehead.

Fig. 13 presents another part of the face, the external ear. (If you prefer not to bother with ears, you may use hair to disguise their absence, as shown in Fig. 12.) You place the ears at the upper end of the jaw, with the bottom of the ear on a line with the tip of the nose and the top extending to fill the second lowest quarter of the head (Fig. 13

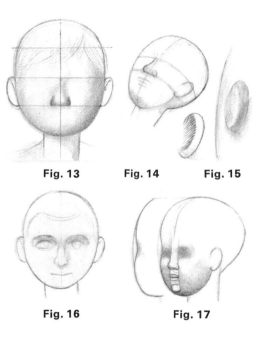

Fig. 13   **Fig. 14**   **Fig. 15**

Fig. 16   **Fig. 17**

and 14). The shape of the ear is given in Fig. 15 in a simple form, which is more or less a rolled oval ending flatly at the cheek.

The next feature to consider is the eyes. They are each imbedded in a depression under the eyebrows (Fig. 16, above). Because of these indentations, the front of the head, which in its basic form was a single curvature, is now subdivided into four zones: the forehead and the two cheek curvatures, which are separated by the fourth zone containing the nose, the mouth and the chin (Fig. 17).

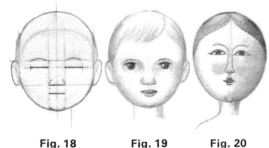

Fig. 18   **Fig. 19**   **Fig. 20**

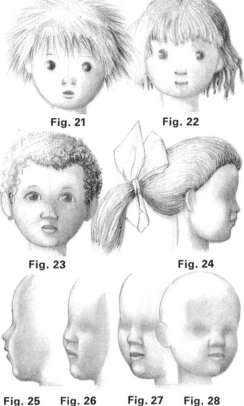

Fig. 21   **Fig. 22**

Fig. 23   **Fig. 24**

Fig. 25   **Fig. 26**   **Fig. 27**   **Fig. 28**

In Fig. 18 the eyes and all other facial details are as they should be on a typical child. The eyebrows are placed on a line just above the top of the ears and at right angles to the vertical axis. The nose is placed at the middle of the lower half of the face. The distance between the eyes should equal the width of the eye itself. Nose, mouth, and chin should all have the same width.

The head itself should receive additional refinement. The curvature at the temple has to be flattened. What we describe here as a norm has nothing to do with your own creativity. You may work as independently as you like. The doll in Fig. 20, for instance, was freely created without following any of the mentioned guide lines. It has something very alluring in its character, and it resembles the head of an antique doll.

The eyes in Illus. 18 have a lifelike expression because they were painted on with nail polish. In Fig. 19, the eyes were not outlined but simply indicated by round pupils and by lines for the upper lids. The line of the lid must partly cover the upper part of the pupil.

The eyes can also be just painted round dots which become more expressive by the addition of a little white dot on each of them (Fig. 21). The facial parts here are simplified, as are the ones in Fig. 22. The hair for Fig. 21 was made from pieces of fur.

The head in Fig. 22 was formed from soft material according to Fig. 1 and 2, page 75.

The back of the head was covered by a wig made from woollen yarn. The face was painted with moistened colored pencils, highlighted by white. The nose was emphasized by stuffing placed inside of the cloth cover. (See pages 74 and 75.)

On heads formed of hard material, the contour of the mouth is given more attention (Fig. 23 and 24). If you look at such a doll in profile (Fig. 24), you can recognize this characteristic. In the turned-away profile (Fig. 25), the chin and the eye depressions particularly have to be observed. Fig. 26, 27 and 28 show three-quarter views. Cheeks, mouth wrinkles, and the sides of the nose

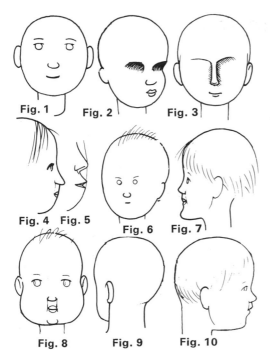

Fig. 1 Fig. 2 Fig. 3

Fig. 4 Fig. 5 Fig. 6 Fig. 7

Fig. 8 Fig. 9 Fig. 10

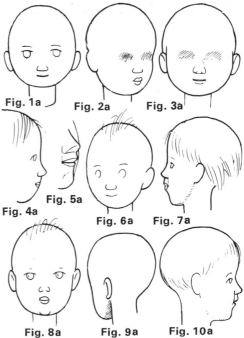

Fig. 1a Fig. 2a Fig. 3a

Fig. 4a Fig. 5a Fig. 6a Fig. 7a

Fig. 8a Fig. 9a Fig. 10a

are the characteristic parts. The sides of the nose meet very gradually with the flat nose bone. Two diagonal cuts will furnish the mouth. The lower lip blends into the chin with very little interruption.

In continuing this chapter, we shall answer the following two questions which are constantly asked by people learning to make doll heads: "Why am I not satisfied with my doll heads? Why is it that they do not appear to me like a child's head?" Figures 1 through 10 here above show incorrect drawings of doll's heads; figures 1a through 10a right above show corrected versions of each head.

Fig. 1: The forehead is too flat and much too short.

Fig. 2: Eye depressions are too deep and the upper edge of each is too sharp.

Fig. 3: The nose is too long, too thin, too edged and too finely chiseled.

Fig. 4: The tip of the nose does not fall diagonally to the upper lip.

Fig. 5: The distance from the upper lip to the nose is too long.

Fig. 6: The facial parts are too small and too close to each other.

Fig. 7: The chin projects too much and is too pointed.

Fig. 8: The rounded cheek should not hang down like a flabby cheek.

Fig. 9: The throat is too thick.

Fig. 10: The throat is placed too far at the back.

The drawings from 1 to 10 show the most common mistakes. In the drawings from 1a to 10a, only described errors were eliminated. The other parts remain unchanged. After you study this chapter completely, you will know how to give your doll heads the characteristics of a child's head.

41

Hard Modelled Heads

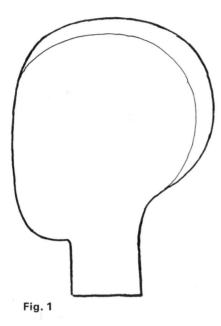

Fig. 1

There are several ways of making heads from model material. First make a paper silhouette of the head (Fig. 1, above). The size of the head depends upon the size of the body. You will need the silhouette as a pattern when forming the head. The inner line shown at the skull on Fig. 1 should be taken into consideration when the doll is to have a thick wig.

Construct a paper core around a stick. You should be able to use the projecting end of the stick as a handle while working. Wind smooth paper around the top of the stick, and glue it into place to make sure it will not unwind again. Now you wrap another layer of paper—soft, thin paper, such as tissue or napkins—over the first layer. Repeat this process several times by wrapping paper piece by piece to build up the core. Then wind sewing yarn very tightly over the paper (Fig. 2). When doing this work, keep comparing the head with the size of your paper pattern, and make sure it is about ¼-inch smaller than the pattern. Then moisten the dry core with glue.

Apply your model material in an average layer of ¼-inch thickness and try to produce the fundamental form of the head described on page 38, Fig. 4 to 6. When this is done (Fig. 3), the head must dry.

Check the hard form. When it is hard enough, measure the equality of both halves of the face. A line in the middle of the face may be helpful (Fig. 4).

After all uneven parts have been corrected, the head must dry again; then you form the facial details (Fig. 5). They may still not look satisfying to you. It is possible that you will have to form the head a fourth or a fifth time. When it comes to forming the nose or the mouth (page 40, Fig. 25 to 28) you can use a small knife, but otherwise you should always use your fingers. Only your fingers can give the soft and smooth form required of a head. The final smoothing and polishing is done last.

A throat ring made from thick paper strips which are wrapped around the neck and glued there (Fig. 5) is helpful in putting a head into the body of a stuffed doll.

Another method of forming the core is to use the shell of an egg. The core is no less solid than the other heads. In fact, all the heads we describe in this book are made to be unbreakable.

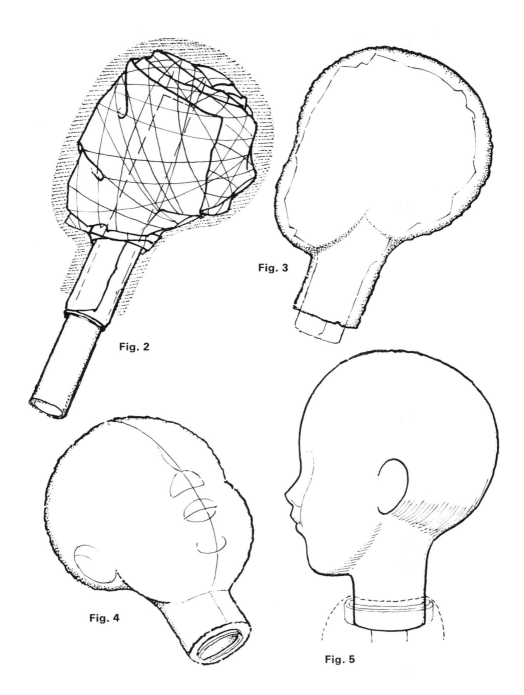

Fig. 2

Fig. 3

Fig. 4

Fig. 5

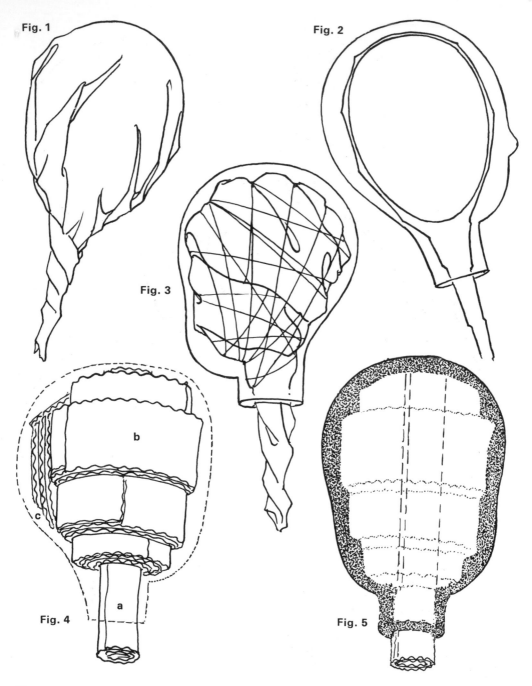

Fig. 1

Fig. 2

Fig. 3

b

c

a

Fig. 4

Fig. 5

44

First obtain the shell of a raw egg that you have emptied. Paste some newspaper over it. Wind the bottom part of the paper into a taper and let everything dry (Fig. 1, page 44).

Cover the wrapped eggshell with a layer of your model material ⅛ to ⅜ inches thick (Fig. 2). The paper taper, which will have become hard in the meantime, will be convenient for holding the head. The upper part of the taper is used as a base for the throat. The final shaping of the head will involve another effort. We do not recommend forming details on small heads such as these. Shaping of the nose and ears are enough to indicate the face.

You can use the eggshell form to make an enlarged head. Begin as you did with the small eggshell head. Then put a few layers of napkins or tissue paper over the first cover as described on page 42, Fig. 2. Using yarn, you wind a net over the head. After this is done, you may give the head a final shape with the help of your sawdust material (Fig. 3).

A head with a corrugated paper core is particularly convenient for a doll of 20 inches or more in length. In this case, corrugated paper will supply the complete core of the head as well as of the throat (Fig. 4). The bottom extends into a handgrip (a). You roll and glue strips of corrugated paper counter-clockwise in a vertical series as shown (b).

In this way, you shape the form of a head. For the back of the head you add a few extra pieces of corrugated paper (c).

Next, you cover the core of the head with your sawdust material and you will get the final form (Fig. 5). Proceed with the details, including the throat ring, as previously described on page 42.

To dry formed heads, stick the handgrip of the head into a bottle. Be sure to have everything shaped and dry before removing the handgrip with a saw cut.

The photographed models on page 46 show the following: Model 1, top left: Fundamental form of a head in egg form.

Model 2, top right: Raw form of an enlarged head in egg form.

Model 3, bottom left: Form in dark sawdust material.

Model 4, bottom right: Sawdust over corrugated paper core, about 4¼ inches high not counting the neck.

Photographs of hard, modelled heads are shown on pages 4, 47, 57, 62, 63, 77, 83, 88 and 89.

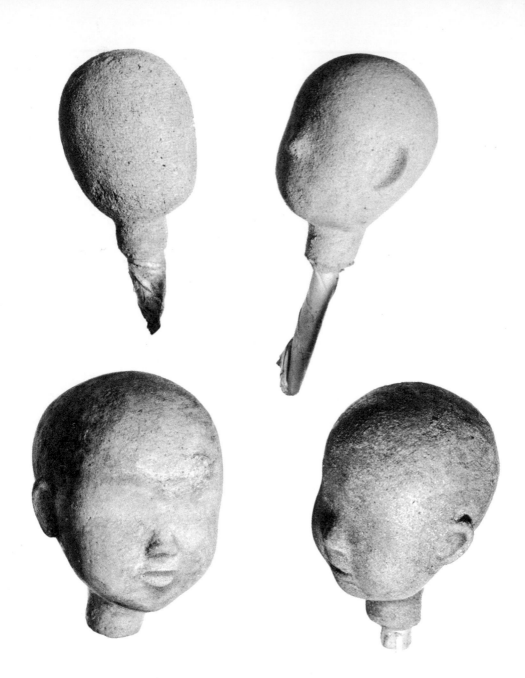

Illus. 10. Heads modelled of sawdust can have a core of paper, eggshell, or cardboard.

Illus. 11. Matrixes were used to cast parts of heads, which are then glued together.

Matrixes for Hollow Heads

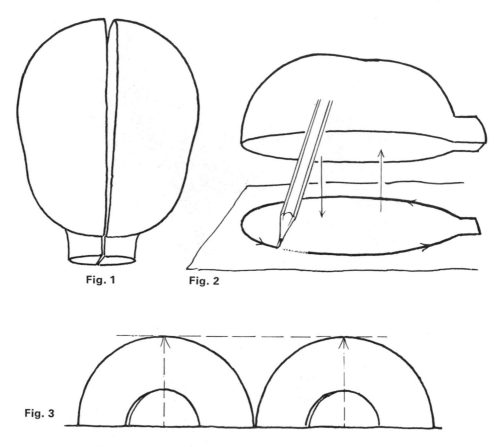

Fig. 1

Fig. 2

Fig. 3

Constructing a matrix (mould) is convenient for making big dolls. Once the mould has been made, it can be used continuously to cast doll heads.

Shape the fundamental form from non-hardening clay or plasticine. With a thin wire, cut through the middle of the form (Fig. 1, above).

Put one half of the head on a sheet of paper and model it into a more final form.

Draw a pencil line (Fig. 2) around this modelled half of the head; then remove it from the paper. Place the second half of the head on the paper and form it so that it conforms exactly to the outline. Both parts of the head have to meet each other exactly when finally put together. To prove that the two halves have the same height, compare the two parts by placing them separately on the table (Fig. 3).

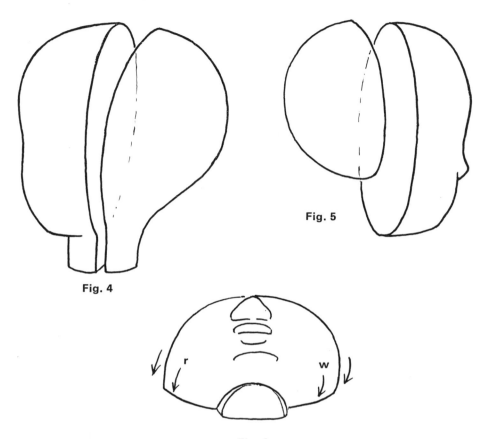

Fig. 5

Fig. 4

Fig. 6

Your model can be cut apart across the skull (Fig. 4) instead of down the face. You can also cut off only the back of the head as shown in Fig. 5. The throat will be established later with sawdust material. In all variations, the cut sections have to match when placed together.

You have to be careful that the curvature of the face is not more acute than the curvature of the cutting level. In Fig. 6, *r* indicates the correct curvature; *w* indicates the wrong

curvature, deviating from the cutting level (indicated by the dotted line) and forming what is known as an undercut. If an undercut exists, it will be difficult to later remove the cast from the mould.

Unless the halves are perfectly symmetrical as in Fig. 1, page 48, each half of the head needs a separate matrix (or mould) made of plaster. Begin by taking one half of the form made from clay and placing it on a flat surface. Completely surround the model by

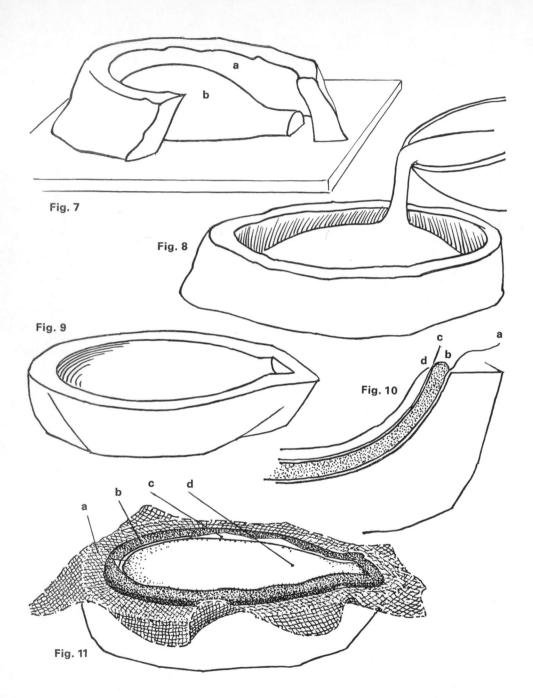

Fig. 7

Fig. 8

Fig. 9

Fig. 10

Fig. 11

a wall of clay that follows the contour (Fig. 7, page 50, which shows only part of the wall). The wall (*a*) should be about ½ inch higher than the highest point of the model (*b*). Fasten the inner side of the wall to the bottom of the flat surface by tightly pressing the clay against it. Brush the exposed bottom surface with liquid soap to avoid having the plaster stick after it is poured and dried.

You can buy plaster easily in hardware stores (at ironmongers). You sift the plaster little by little into a bowl which is three-quarters filled with water, until you can see a little hill above the water. Stir the mixture slightly with a spatula until it becomes creamy. Pour the first layer of the mass slowly over your model (Fig. 8). Bowl and spatula have to be washed and cleaned immediately. Pour another layer of the plaster into the tub formed by the clay walls. Repeat until you have the tub entirely filled.

After about 20 minutes the plaster will be a compact mass and can be lifted from the clay form after you remove the retaining wall. Wash the plaster form and let it dry. When finished (Fig. 9), it can be smoothed with steel wool and painted with a water-tight cover such as lacquer. Now you have your matrix, in which you cast the sawdust material.

To fill the matrix with sawdust material for the head form, you now apply at the inner wall of the plaster the following material, layer by layer (Fig. 10):

(*a*): a gauze sieve which can be lifted by its edges. This way the finished bowl can be taken out easily from the matrix.

(*b*): sawdust mass, which gives the head its substance.

(*c*): cellophane, which isolates the model material from the next layer.

(*d*): a plaster layer, which prevents the sawdust material from shrinking at the inner side.

Fig. 11 shows the filled mould after you have followed the sequence of work which is explained in this paragraph. First, put a piece of gauze sieve on an even surface, knead the model material into a flat cake, put it on the gauze and squeeze it with the ball of your thumb and a spatula, working from the middle to the sides, until it has the thickness of ½ inch. Together with the gauze you sink the model material into the matrix and press both together against the walls until they are tightly connected. Cut away the left over mass at the edges. Furnish the inside with a thin layer of cellophane paper and over this apply your plaster with a painter's brush. As soon as the plaster is hard, you lift the edges of the gauze with the filling and remove the entire cast from the matrix. Then remove the gauze. Let the sawdust cast become hard. When the plaster layer is hard, remove it.

The entire process, from making the matrix to casting it with model material, has to be done with the other half of the head. Then, to finish the work, the edges of the two separate casts have to be smoothed with sandpaper and pasted together with your model material or glue. Now the last details can be worked out. Furnish the head with ears, smooth the finished form and apply a water-tight coat of color or lacquer.

The photographed models on page 47 show hollow heads made from matrixes. They illustrate the different ways to divide the original clay head.

Wigs for a Doll

Fig. 1 and 2: You see a line (*a*) which indicates the hairline. The shape of the wig will be determined by this line as well as by the line on the back of the head.

You can use various types of fur for making a wig. With a razor blade, cut little pieces and paste them directly onto the head. Long hair may be cut in clumps from the fur and then glued onto your model. When doing this work the hair-bed has to be moistened with glue first, using a small spatula or knife.

You may prefer to form the wig first from little pieces you have sewn together, and then paste it as a whole creation on to the head of the doll. Preferably you should form the wig bit by bit around the skull's contour, sewing the pieces together with a fur needle, using the underside of the fur. Be sure to use a spatula or a brush when applying the glue to the head.

Fig. 3: Crimean lambskin is very convenient for making a wig. It is a woollen material which is similar to lamb's wool. As can be seen in the illustration, this material is aptly applied on a little Negro doll.

Fig. 4: A little cap made from tulle or another light fabric is a good framework for a wig which is made from cut hair. At the forehead of the doll you fold the edge of the material inside and hold it with pins exactly where you wish the onset of the hair. Pull the material towards the neck (*a*) and fix it there in the same way. Folding the material as shown, sew it with back-stitches where it crosses the back of the neck. Any material left over can be removed with scissors. The cap is glued to the head after the hairs are sewn to it.

Fig. 5: Using a double strip of tissue paper or a strip of tulle, you take the hairs and spread them in a thin, even layer over the paper or cloth. Then sew a seam down the middle with a sewing machine. While doing this you can hold the hairs loosely between your fingers. In the second step, (Fig. 5a) you fold the layer of hair on the seam and place a second seam next to the first one. Now the hair cannot be pulled out. If you moisten the hair, you will be able to bend it without any difficulty. After that you pull the paper strip away and sew the hair to a tulle cap, which you then glue to the head.

Fig. 6: Wigs imitating cut hair can be produced from nylon fibre. This is a fine substitute for any real hair. You can easily obtain this material in lengths of 10 inches. If you buy it in its natural color, you may dye it if you wish. The results are best when you dye the hair and the little cap together. In our illustration, the hair is sewn to tulle strips (using only one seam instead of two as in Fig. 5a) and then sewn to the cap at three places—on the back of the head, in the middle, and at the forehead.

When you are finished with the wig, the hair has to be cut. Don't cut it too short, otherwise it will become difficult to handle with a comb and brush. If you keep it long, you can fix it easily and make any desired hairdo you wish. Tulle strips sewn with

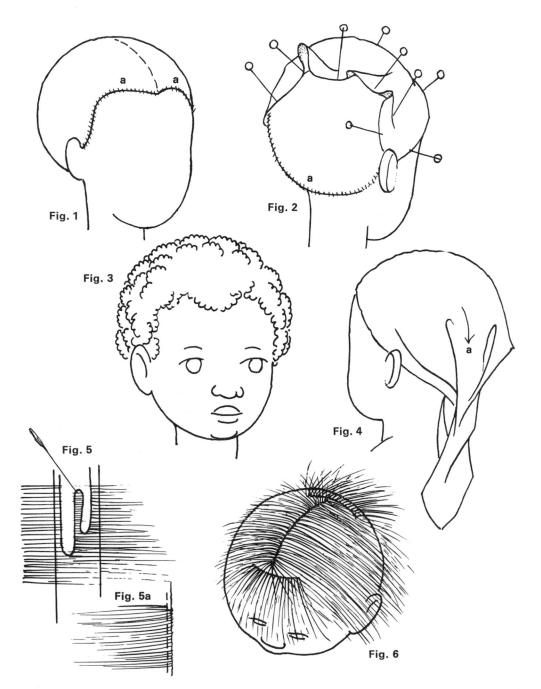

Fig. 1

Fig. 2

Fig. 3

Fig. 4

Fig. 5

Fig. 5a

Fig. 6

53

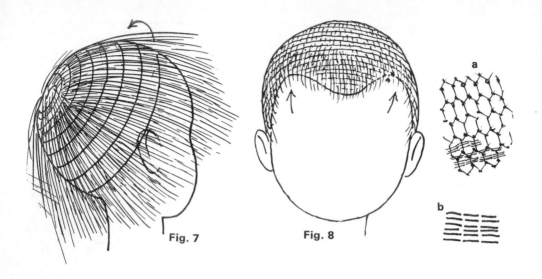

Fig. 7

Fig. 8

a

b

wool, cotton-wool, silk, soft cords or other material besides real hair are also handled very conveniently with comb and brush.

Fig. 7: On large heads you can use a hair-band (a tulle strip sewn with hair) of about 11 feet in length wound like a spiral. You sew it with overcast stitches around the skull. The hair will fall loosely over the whole head.

Fig. 8, above: This illustration shows a crocheted cap (a) covered with span stitches (b). This is a stitch worked with a needle to imitate hair. We recommend this kind of wig for short-haired dolls. When sewing the cap at the head you should pull it backwards at the temple so that no material can be seen later. The stitch imitates smooth hair.

Fig. 9: This shows a crocheted cap with knotted "Smyrna" knots from wool (Fig. 10). You may cut the hair to any length.

Fig. 11, a to d: Loop wigs without a cap are recommended for hard heads. Wind the yarn around a strip of cardboard (a), in which you have first cut a notch at top and bottom. The width of the cardboard should be the length of hair you have decided upon.

The loops are kept together with a piece of yarn which is first covered with glue (b). Then the cardboard is removed by unlooping the yarn from the notches and pulling the cardboard out. The loops (c) are now placed piece by piece at the head with the fringe-end facing down (d). Cut through the loops last.

Fig. 12: To make loop wigs for soft heads, wind the yarn around a ruler or pencil, sew the loops together with seam stitches, pull the ruler away and sew the wig by its seam-line on to the head.

Fig. 13: Looped wigs can also be made on a little cap (see Fig. 4, page 53). You sew double-threaded yarn at the head, making loop by loop, in a spiral-like manner. Keep holding the cap with your left hand and press the loops downwards. To avoid any sliding away of the loops, the completed cap has to be pasted over the head. This process is suitable for big heads (Juten doll, see page 77).

Fig. 14, page 56: To make tassel wigs, a cardboard strip as wide as the length of hair you have decided upon has to be wrapped with wool yarn, silk yarn or anything similar.

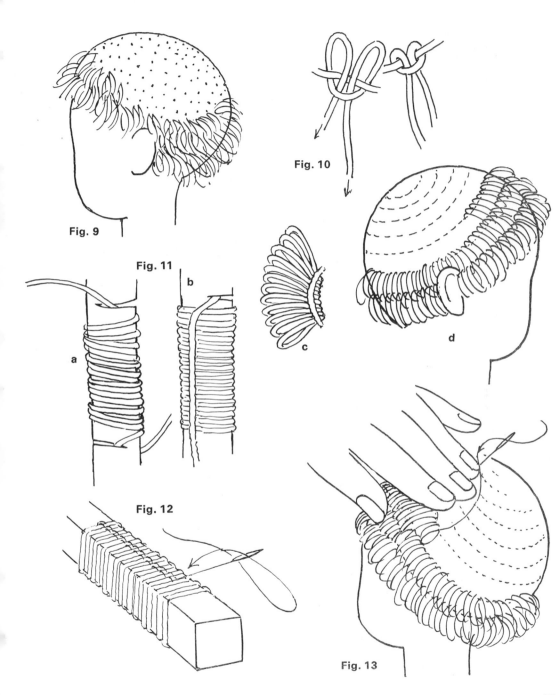

Fig. 9

Fig. 10

Fig. 11

a

b

c

d

Fig. 12

Fig. 13

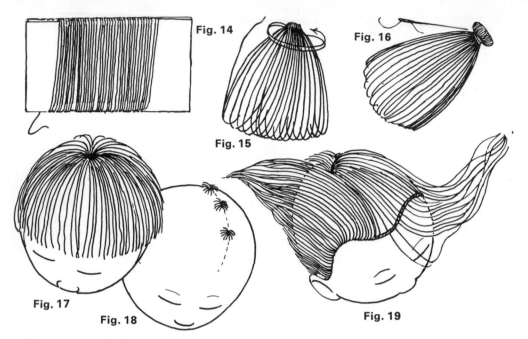

Fig. 14

Fig. 16

Fig. 15

Fig. 17

Fig. 18

Fig. 19

Fig. 15: Strip the loops off and hold them together with the end of the yarn used.

Fig. 16: The hairs are kept together at the top, sewn up with back-stitches and the loops are opened with a cut.

Fig. 17: The tassel produced as in Fig. 16 has to be sewn at the crown, where the squeezed knot is fastened inwards. Then give the wig the haircut you desire.

Fig. 18: On tassels which are too thick, the knot looks unnatural. You can avoid this by distributing three tassels instead of one over the middle of the head.

Fig. 19: For a pony-tail hairdo you have to sew a cord along the hairline (Fig. 1, page 53). The hair should be evenly distributed. After the cord is sewn to the hairline the hair can be pulled back over the cord and tied with a bow.

Examples of wigs on our models are found on the following pages.

Page 57, modelled hard heads: (top left) The hair is drawn with a colored pencil and

painted over with a damp brush; (top right) curled lamb's wool, glued directly on to the head in small bunches; (middle) loop wig made from curled wool, produced as shown in Fig. 11, page 55; (bottom right) lamb's wool is glued directly on to the head in little pieces.

Page 4: Nylon fibre. As described on page 54, Fig. 7.

Page 20: (Left) Curled wool sewn on in any desired fashion; (right) Tassel wig made from shiny yarn.

Page 81: (Left) Icelandic lamb's wool divided into 3 strips; (right) Curled wool.

Page 88: Plush, glued on.

Bookcover: Synthetic fibre. Three hair-bands were used as described on page 53, Fig. 5 and 6.

Illus. 12. Hair for hard heads can be painted on, or wigs can be glued on.

Mannequin Dolls

Every young girl is pleased to clothe her dolls and sew dresses for them. Mannequin dolls, which can be made in any size, are particularly suitable for this and the creation of such a doll can be very exciting.

There are special requirements for this kind of doll. She must not be too small, but should have a size of at least 10 inches. You should be able to dress her without any difficulties. Therefore, her arms must be movable and the feet should be free-standing. In other words, she must not stand on a pedestal. Her figure must have good proportions; only then will a dress be most effective. All of these prerequisites are best fulfilled on a hard, modelled doll.

Fig. 1 to 3, page 59, show the proportions of a 13½-year-old girl. All measurements are dependent upon the size of the head, and they can be calculated in accordance with the graph pattern. First you must note that the total height of the body equals the length of six heads. The average width of the body equals one head, with the waist being smaller and the hips wider.

Make a framework of three little wooden sticks and three strips cut from strong cardboard to support the model material. From the illustrations you can see how the length of the sticks and cardboard strips are related to the final doll. The sticks are approximately ¼ inch thick. They do not have to be absolutely well-rounded. If they are notched (a) or covered with glue first, your model material will stick to them more firmly.

Put the sticks and pieces of cardboard on a table and glue them together as shown in the illustrations. (The rod (b) projecting from the shoulder is inserted later and will be explained further on in the text.)

The finished framework will stand in two holes that you make in a small piece of board. Therefore, the sticks for the feet should each have the additional length as shown in Fig. 1, c. Also an additional length of the torso stick should extend from the head (d), so you can use this as a handle while modelling the doll.

The contours of the mannequin doll can be seen in its three main plane views. Your primary concern is to make a simple reproduction of the body areas. The shapes remain round and are tapered only when coming toward the wrist of the hand and toward the feet. Model the head, body, legs and feet.

While you are modelling the body, insert the small round rod (b) shown in Fig. 1 to 3 and in diagrams on page 60. This will enable you to add movable arms, which are modelled separately. (The rotating joint at each shoulder is marked in a vertical line on Fig. 4, page 60.) The small round rod through the body and upper arms serves as a temporary axle. The rod has to be placed toward the back of the torso, below the top of the shoulder.

The inner framework (core) of an arm

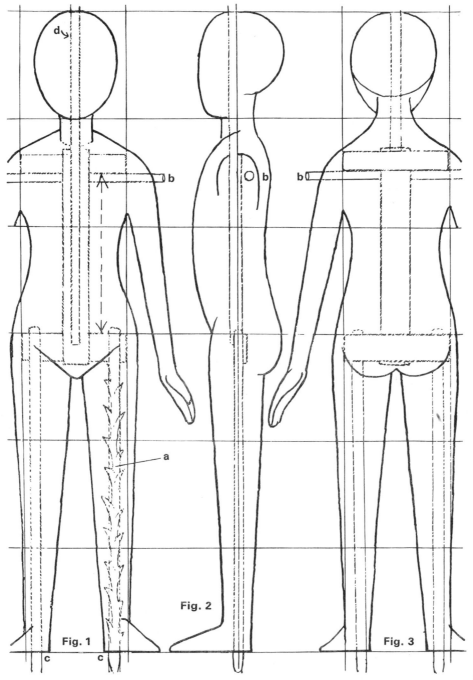

Fig. 1

Fig. 2

Fig. 3

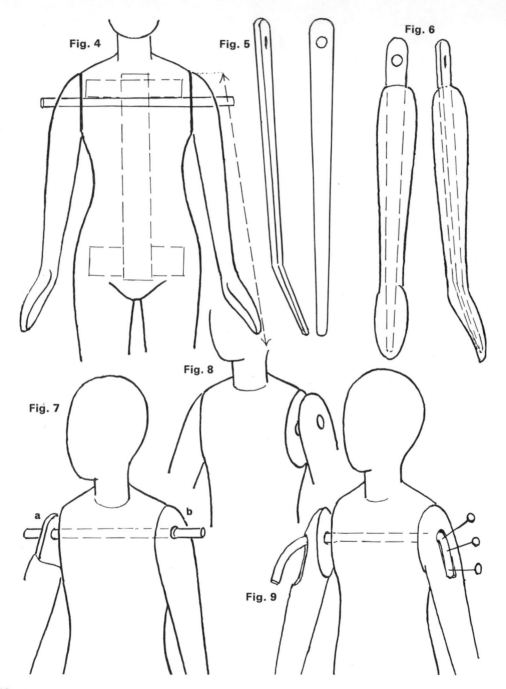

Fig. 4

Fig. 5

Fig. 6

Fig. 7

Fig. 8

a
b

Fig. 9

with hand can be cut from cardboard of average thickness. In length this should be from the shoulder to the middle of the thigh. This cardboard frame has to have a hole at the top (Fig. 5) through which to pass your axle rod.

Now, you begin to form the arms and hands with your model material, leaving the upper end free (Fig. 6). Attach the arms to the rod you have put through the shoulders of the doll (Fig. 7, *a*) and then finish modelling the arms (*b*).

After the material is hard, you remove the rod by rotating it with a pair of pliers. Then cut the arms from the torso with a vertical saw cut (Fig. 8).

You connect the arms and body again with a piece of solid (not hollow) rubber tubing (Fig. 9) inserted by turning it slowly through the holes. Each end of the rubber is sunk into a groove, made with a knife, in the upper arm, and then glued. Hold the ends in place with pins until the glue sets. Pull the rubber tight, but do not make it too taut so that you can rotate the arms moderately. Then, fill the groove with model material again. (Solid rubber tubing is available from rubber products dealers.)

The photograph on page 63 shows two models of mannequin dolls. The one on the left has the proportions of a 13-year-old girl and the one on the right represents a 5-year-old girl. The fundamental forms were smoothed with sandpaper, covered with two coats of paint (casein or acrylic), and polished with a rag. While you can dispense with a painting on light-colored sawdust (pine wood) you can give your forms skin tone by using colored pencils. A coat of wax (varnish is too shiny) will safeguard against moisture.

Mannequin dolls in show-windows usually have no fully detailed faces. The attention of people should be drawn to the dress, so your dolls should also be without facial details. However, if you care to, you may add features as on the dressed doll shown. The eyes and the mouth were painted with opaque color and covered with nail polish. The wig is made from woollen yarn glued directly on to the head.

If there should be any difficulties with the standing position of the doll, you may drill a small hole into the soles of the feet and then stick the doll on two nails which you have driven through a small piece of board. Of course, these nails should not be seen after the doll has been placed in its standing position.

Illus. 13. Instructions for making these disc-jointed dolls are in next chapter.

Illus. 14. Mannequin dolls have jointed arms made with rubber tubing.

Dolls with Disc Joints

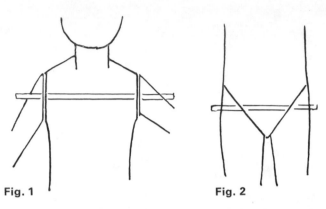

Fig. 1   Fig. 2

These dolls have movable shoulders and hip joints. They must be able to sit and stand freely, no matter whether the doll is stuffed or formed from hard material. One of the problems which has to be considered is the mechanics of the hip joints.

It is possible to turn the legs like the arms around an axle which is placed through the body (Fig. 1 and 2, above). However, while the turning point of the arms is balanced *outside* of the torso, the turning point for the legs has to be built *into* the torso by using diagonal saw cuts. Any other solution would give a distortion between the lower body and the upper thigh.

Imagine the hip joint of the doll as a spool which is turning itself around its middle axis (Fig. 3). This spool is divided into three parts by two imagined diagonal saw cuts (Fig. 4). The middle part belongs to the torso, the parts on the outer sides to the movable legs.

Looking at the doll in profile, you can recognize the turn of the leg forward in a standing position (Fig. 5). But the leg must also turn to the side, in order to show a sitting position. Fig. 6 and 7 show the legs turned on their axle so that the doll can sit with separated thighs and with feet turned sidewards.

If the two cuts on the spool were made to face each other in a right angle (Fig. 4a), the legs would have to be spread so wide in their sitting position that the feet would be placed in an unnatural position on the floor (Fig. 6). You avoid this undesirable feature by dividing the spool in such a manner that both saw cuts will face each other at equal, acute angles (Fig. 3 and 4). The more acute the angles are, the less the legs can be spread when putting the doll in a sitting position.

The photograph on page 62 shows two models of hard, modelled dolls with disc joints. At the left, you see the fundamental form of the body. It has movable joints and a head which can be turned. (How to make the movable head will be explained in a later chapter.) At the right is a finished, painted doll. A wig made from wool yarn was glued directly on to the head.

The photographs on pages 4, 83, 88, and the book cover give examples of stuffed dolls with disc joints. Such dolls are dealt with in a later chapter.

Twig dolls may also be jointed, as shown on page 5. For the hip joint, a hole was drilled through the branch, which was then cut diagonally. For a better anchoring of the rubber tubing, the grooves were filled with model material. Shoes and gloves were modelled separately, so that they can be taken off.

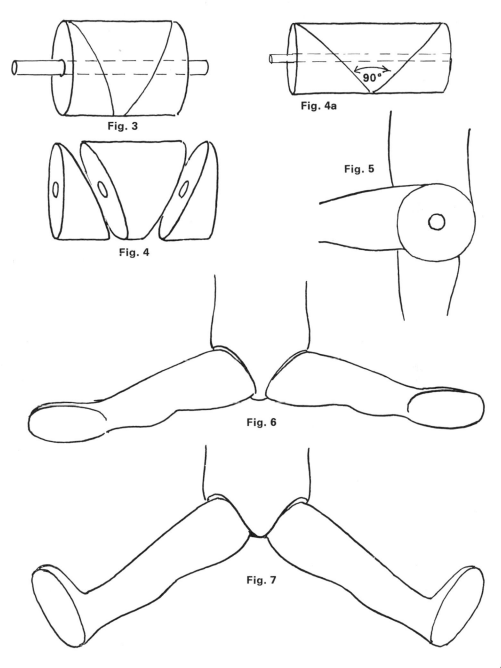

Fig. 3

Fig. 4a

90°

Fig. 4

Fig. 5

Fig. 6

Fig. 7

Modelled Dolls with Joints

First you build the basic framework (Fig. 1, page 67). The spool used to produce the hip joint (Fig. 3 and 4, page 65) will supply the pelvis and the upper part of each leg. You form this spool from model material. A dowel approximately ¼ inch thick has to be pushed through the middle of the spool while the material is still soft. You can also use a pencil or a knitting needle instead of a dowel.

When the spool is hard, remove the dowel and indicate with a pencil the two diagonal lines necessary, then saw the spool into three parts as described in the previous chapter. Drill three holes in the divided spool—one at the top of the pelvic portion (Fig. 1, *b*), and one at the bottom of each leg portion (Fig. 1, *c*). Insert dowels into these holes and firmly glue them in. Lightly glue a dowel (Fig. 1, *a*) for the shoulders to the rod which forms the backbone of the torso. This is the basic framework for your model (Fig. 1). (The rods are shown here as notched to hold the model material better.)

While the head and torso have to be modelled together, the legs and arms are produced separately. The feet will be supplied with a cardboard sole (Fig. 1 a, page 67) by sticking the leg skeletons through the cardboard. (Following the dimensions of our example, the length of the sole will be 1⅛ inches.)

Build up the torso and the leg forms as shown in Fig. 2. (Re-insert temporary dowels in the spool holes while modelling.) Here are the measurements we used: The length of the doll is 8 inches; head and throat together are 1½ inches. The length of the spool is 1½ inches, while its diameter is 1 inch. The leg rod from the spool down to the sole is 2¾ inches long. The backbone rod coming from the top of the spool up to the skull will have a length of 4¾ inches; from the spool to the shoulder-axle dowel the backbone rod is 2 inches long. These measurements can, of course, have any variation. With the help of the graph pattern, the doll can be enlarged into any size you desire.

An additional length of backbone dowel should be left at the head for handling your work. You should also leave an extra length of dowel at each foot to stick into a board while drying the model. These extra lengths of dowel are removed with a saw before final finishing of the doll.

To make the arms, you work step by step with the model as explained by Fig. 4 to 9, page 60.

Fig. 3 diagrams the finished doll. The joints provide movable arms and legs joined to the body by rubber tubing (described on page 61) at the shoulders and hips. To prevent the undesirable turning of the legs in a 360-degree circle, you can add a small ridge of model material where legs and back are connected. (Fig. 6, page 73.)

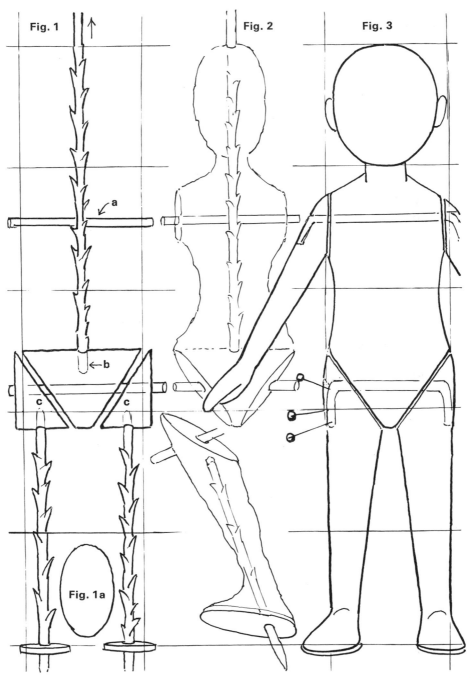

Fig. 1

a

Fig. 1a

b

c   c

Fig. 2

Fig. 3

67

Shaping Legs and Arms

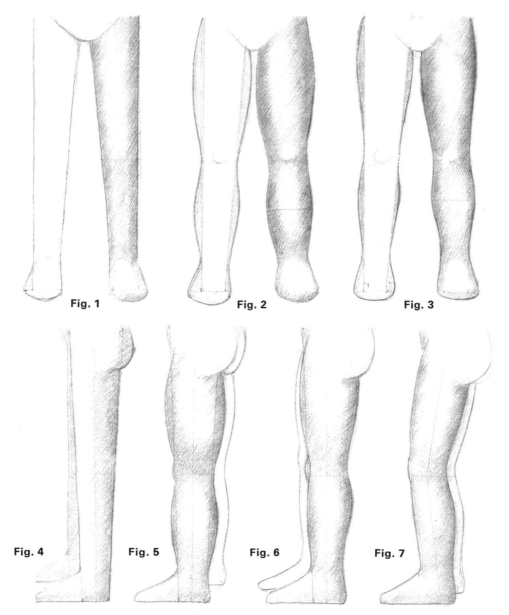

Fig. 1   Fig. 2   Fig. 3

Fig. 4   Fig. 5   Fig. 6   Fig. 7

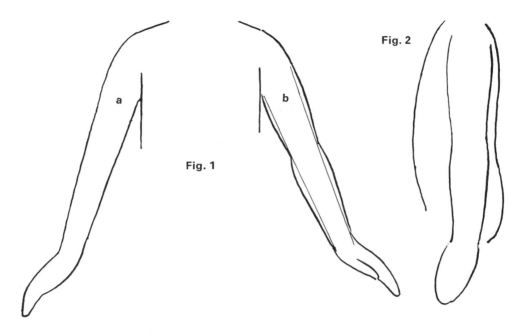

Fig. 2

a

Fig. 1

b

If you are not satisfied with the fundamental form of the leg, which is shown in
Fig. 1, page 68 as a tapered tube, the question
for you will be: How far can you go in
sculpturing your own leg shapes? Comparing
your doll with a doll made in a factory is not
necessary. You have to find a solution in
between which allows you to replace the
tube-like form with a more natural form,
without becoming too realistic.

Fig. 2 and 3 both show the basic form
enhanced by the curvatures of natural
muscles. In Fig. 2 the muscles of the thighs
and shin bones have been shaped to convex
forms, each of which shows the widest part
in the middle of the curve. In Fig. 3, however, not the middle, but the top half of each
curve displays the greatest span. This con-
formation is closer to nature.

Fig. 4 is a view from the side of the form in
Fig. 1.

The disadvantage of the form shown in
Fig. 2 is particularly noticeable in the side

view, Fig. 5. Here the lower part of the thigh
appears too clumsy.

The form in Fig. 6 is the side view of Fig. 3.
The greater width on the upper half of the
thigh and on the upper half of the shin
create the curves that show a perfectly
shaped knee.

Bending the knee joint a little (Fig. 7) will
loosen the tightness of a standing leg. This
mannerism of a somewhat unsure stance is
typical of small children. You can apply this
characteristic very well in forming your own
doll.

For the basic form of the arm (Fig. 1, *a*,
above), you will use a tube which is tapered
toward the wrist, then bent over into a flat
hand. The muscles of the arm (*b*) are shaped
in curves in almost the same way as the legs.
At the top half of the upper arm you
can recognize the area where the most
strength of an arm should be put (delta
muscle). Fig. 2 shows the arm when it is
relaxed and the torso is seen in profile.

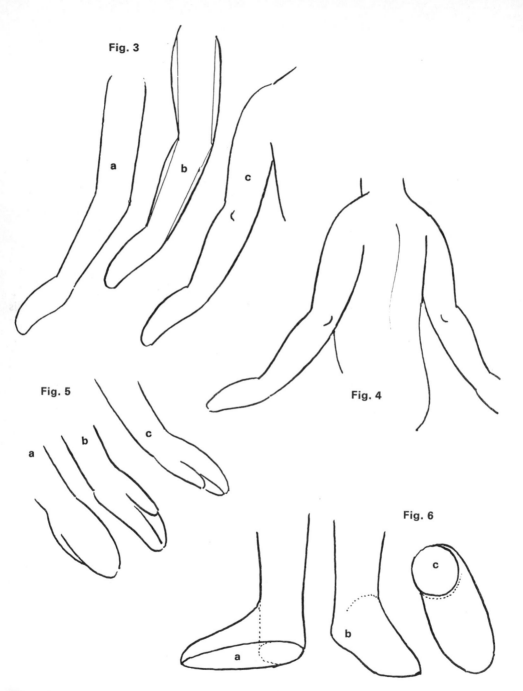

Fig. 3

a   b   c

Fig. 5

a   b   c

Fig. 4

Fig. 6

c

b

a

Fig. 3, *a* to *c*, is to be compared with Fig. 4 to 6, page 60. Here the elbow is shown slightly bent. Diagram *b* shows the effect bending the elbow has upon the shape of the muscles. While the outline of the back of the arm arcs in a smooth bow towards the wrist, the front of the arm shows the bulging muscles. This is a side view. Diagram *c* shows the arm from the rear, while Fig. 4 pictures the bent arm in a diagonal view of the body.

In modelling the hands (Fig. 5), do not strive to obtain very many details; the hands of the doll will simply look like they have gloves on. Only the thumb will be clearly indicated. Diagram *a* shows the top view, *b* is a three-quarter view and *c* is a side view.

The feet (Fig. 6) are made simply, too, without toes. The form of the foot will be outlined by shaping a flat sole (*a*) and then the heel (*b*). (Diagram *c* is the top view of a foot.)

You soon recognize distorted parts on a doll, such as: wrongly placed or overdone stomach muscles, or feet and hands tapered too strongly. The shape of a child's body is important; less profile and more softness of the form are desirable.

The smaller the doll, the simpler its forms must be. Eight or 10 inches is considered to be the maximum measurement if the details of the doll are to be kept limited. You will obtain a more skilful feeling for shaping a large doll when making a model from hard material than when using a stuffing material for arms and legs. Therefore, in the next chapter we will present another procedure for making jointed dolls from modelling materials.

A Fully Developed Jointed Doll

With the help of a graph pattern (see page 59), you draw an enlarged profile picture of the doll you plan to make (Fig. 1, page 73). The arms, while superimposed here, should be drawn on a separate sheet of paper. After drawing the leg-and-torso sketch, you cut it out (omitting the head and arms, but including a hanger (a) at the bottom) and trace it twice on to a thick cardboard by outlining it. Cut the two outlined shapes out with scissors. Now you have two cardboard silhouettes of the legs and torso. Use the same process to make a basic framework for the arms (see page 70, Fig. 3, a).

Similarly, cut two silhouettes of the head and throat together from the cardboard and with the help of your model material, glue the two pieces on to a short piece of dowel (c, Fig. 2).

Make two holes—one at the shoulder and the other at the hip—through each of the torso-leg cardboard frames (Fig. 3). Insert two dowels, one at the hips and one at the shoulders. They will serve as axles while you model the doll.

In Fig. 4, which shows the back view of the nearly completed doll, the two cardboard cut-outs can be recognized in a longitudinal view (a and b). The model material (hatched lines) has to be applied separately on to each cardboard cut-out, and the two modelled cut-outs have to be dried before they are put together. But both parts have to be symmetrical. Using the hanger (Fig. 1, a) the torso can be hung for drying. In the meantime, the head and throat are modelled as shown (Fig. 5).

After the head and throat have been made and everything is dry, the torso pieces and the head have to be put together with sawdust material in between (dark hatched lines, Fig. 4). Temporarily, small dowels have to be pulled through the torso at the hips and shoulders as shown. (The shoulder dowel goes in front of the head dowel.) The whole model has to be tied together with a piece of yarn, and then hung for drying. Then the axle dowels are removed.

The arms (d), which are to be made and connected with the torso as described on page 60, Fig. 4 to 9, simply have to be attached to the doll. However, the legs have to be separated from the torso with diagonal saw cuts (e) as described on page 65, Fig. 4. Then, all parts have to be worked over and smoothed. The hangers are removed, the grooves are cut for anchoring the rubber tubing, the feet are supplied with cardboard or imitation leather soles glued on, and the limbs are connected with the body as described on page 61.

To avoid any undesirable backward turning of the legs, the rear of each leg gets a small raised edge of sawdust material where the legs and back are connected (hatched line in Fig. 6).

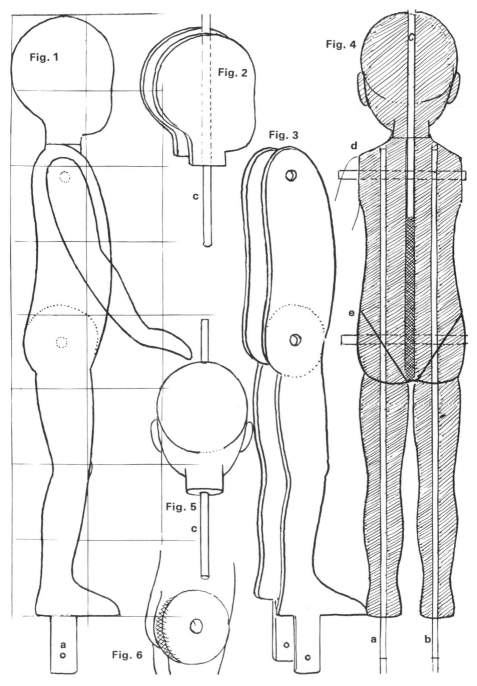

Fig. 1

Fig. 2

c

Fig. 3

Fig. 4

c

d

e

Fig. 5

c

Fig. 6

a
o

a

b

Semi-hard Heads Covered with Cloth

Since we will soon consider the making of stuffed, jointed dolls, this chapter will deal with the construction of heads especially made for stuffed dolls so they can be inserted and moved.

First you form a ball from fine shavings (excelsior), which is then wound with yarn (Fig. 1, page 75).

The first cloth cover (Fig. 2) is made from a thin material, which is extended to form a neck (b) and is tied off at the throat (a). The neck is then wrapped with strips of the cloth until the desired thickness is obtained. Then the overlapping edge is sewn into a seam.

The indentations which will later form the eye sockets, mouth, and neckline are made with yarn which is pulled through the head as shown by the dotted lines in Fig. 3 and then tied at the back (a).

The full expression of the face is obtained by adding a nose, lips, slightly bowed cheeks and a softly modelled chin. This shaping can be done with blotting paper, which has to be glued on to the face in small pieces (Fig. 4). (Fig. 3 shows a brush used to apply glue.)

As an alternative, the face can be covered with sawdust material (Fig. 5). Here, you are able to soften the eye depressions (a), or uneven stitches on the neckline (b). You can also form the curve of the back of the head much better (c). The cloth covering the head has to be moistened with glue before being covered with your modelling material.

As a second cover, a woman's stocking or tricot material can be used (Fig. 6). Your material should have the natural color of the body. Glue has to be spread on the front of the head beginning from the hairline (a) to the middle of the throat (b). In the event that the glue should moisten the material too much, let it be absorbed before working any further on the doll. Put your square piece of stocking material diagonally (c) over the head. Pull it strongly backwards over the head, and pin it at the back. Carefully mould the material over the glue-moistened face, covering the yarn stitches, etc. to form the doll's facial features. Cut away any extra folds. Continue to manoeuvre the material until the head and throat are tightly covered with stocking cloth; then pull any leftover folds up to the scalp and glue them there. A wig will cover these later. This kind of cover softens the sharp features of the doll's face.

Finally, wind a throat ring (Fig. 6) made from strong cord around the neck, winding the cord a few times and then sewing it on. This will help to hold the movable head well, after it has been stuck into the torso of your doll. A model of a doll with a semi-hard head in a stuffed body is shown on page 76.

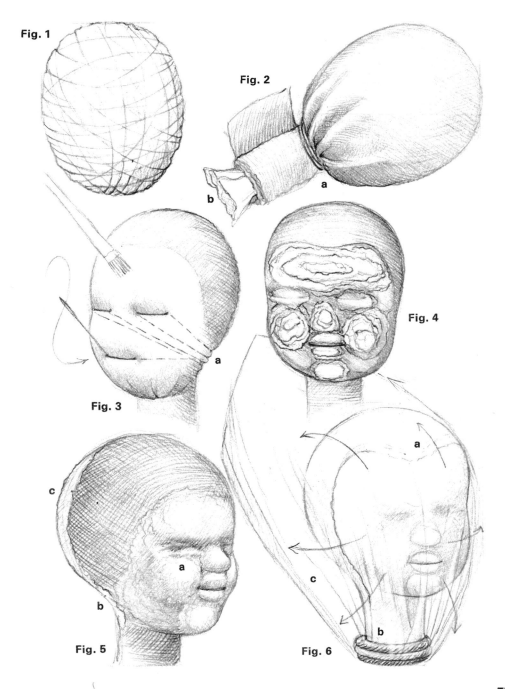

Fig. 1

Fig. 2

a

b

Fig. 3

a

Fig. 4

a

Fig. 5

c

a

b

Fig. 6

a

c

b

75

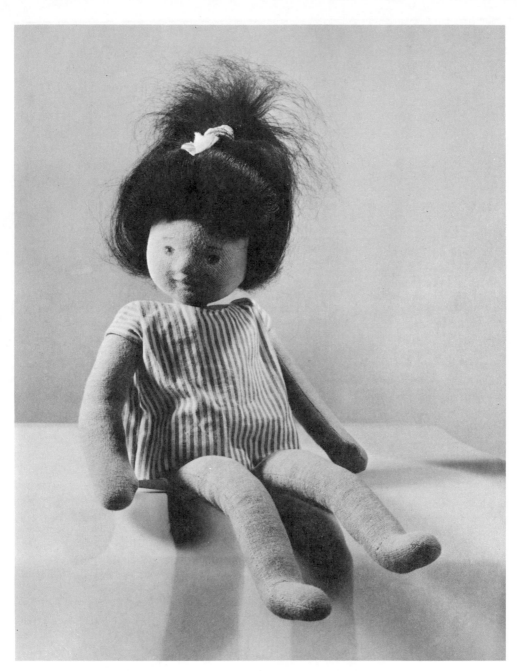

Illus. 15. This semi-hard head is attached to a cloth body made from a pattern.

Illus. 16. The Juten doll is also sewn from a pattern, but it has a hard head.

Stuffed Dolls from a Pattern

If you want to make this kind of doll you must already be familiar with working with patterns. To enlarge any paper pattern shown here, trace it on graph paper. Then take another piece of paper the size you want your pattern to be and draw a grid with the same number of larger squares on it. Copy each line as it appears on the small square on to the large squares. Use this pattern to cut out your material.

Stuffing the material will be new for you. Re-used wool, cotton, gauze, or used nylon stockings are most convenient for stuffing these dolls. The stuffing of dolls is a work which requires patience, care, and a feeling for form. Any lumps or any empty spots cannot be made to disappear once the doll is fully stuffed. Carelessness and uneven stuffing can ruin the best paper pattern and your design. Therefore, you always have to start at the joints first and then push the material in small portions into the holes, distributing it immediately with your fingers and if necessary with a pointed object.

Always begin to stuff by coming from the middle and pushing against the walls. When you stuff the hands, the stuffing material has to be pushed with a thick knitting needle into the thumb. If you fill arms and legs loosely, the doll can be seated better. Once the limb cover is stuffed, you close it with pins, roll it on the table so that uneven spots are corrected, then sew it to the body with even stitches.

The head is the last part to be added. Remember that the dimensions of the head should be proportional to the dimensions of the body (see page 26). When the head, including the wig, is finished, it has to be pushed into the opening of the throat and there connected with the body. It is up to you if you want to have a movable head or not. If you decide to give your doll a movable head (hard, modelled or semi-hard), you have to supply it with a throat ring (Fig. 5, page 43 and Fig. 6, page 75), which will prevent the head from slipping out of the body. If the head is to be unmovable, the head has to be sewn to the body with backstitches at the throat. In such a case, you would use a semi-hard head without the throat ring.

An easy first project is to make the head and body from one piece of cloth material. (In cutting a pattern do not forget to leave a margin of cloth around the paper outline to serve as a seam.) The paper pattern for the tubelike head-body is shown in Fig. 1, page 79. Cut two layers of cloth, placing the dotted line *a* on the fold of your material, and sew the seam at *b*. C remains open to serve as a hole for stuffing. D has to be sewn. The wig will cover this part later. The head has to be stuffed to a firmly rounded ball which is then wrapped at the area (*e*) where the throat joins the body. The body should be less firmly stuffed. Sew the small hole at the bottom of the doll between the place where the legs will be (see stitches in Fig. 1, *c*).

Following the paper pattern in Fig. 2, cut out the legs, two layers of cloth for each one. Make your seams, leaving the tops open. After stuffing the legs, sew the top hole together. The legs have to be pushed into the body and sewn to it with running stitches. The feet (*e*) have to be indicated with backstitches.

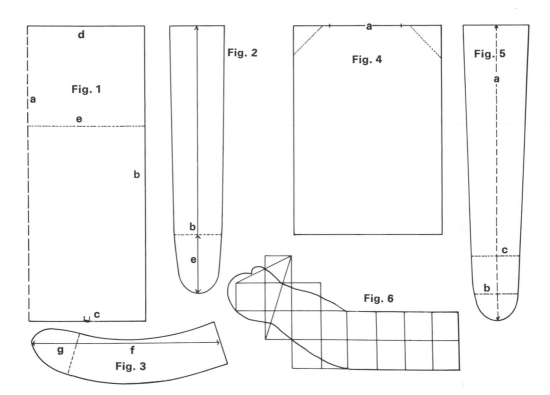

Fig. 1
Fig. 2
Fig. 3
Fig. 4
Fig. 5
Fig. 6

The arms of your doll are made in the same manner as the legs, following the pattern in Fig. 3. They have to be placed loosely at the body and sewn. They can be bent slightly if desired. Hands are indicated by winding yarn around the wrist.

Examples of dolls made in this way are shown on page 81. The model on the left has a total length of 16 inches. Head and body cover together have a size of $8\frac{1}{2} \times 3\frac{1}{4}$ inches. Legs and feet are $7\frac{1}{2} \times 1\frac{3}{8}$ inches. The arm (*f* in Fig. 3, above) is $5 \times 1\frac{1}{8}$ inches. The face is painted with moistened colored pencils. The wig is made from fur. In the model on the right, the hair is made from curled wool.

Next, here are instructions for making a doll with a semi-hard movable head. Fig. 4, this page, gives the paper pattern (without seam allowances) for the body cover. The rectangle should be $5\frac{3}{4}$ inches by $4\frac{1}{4}$ inches. Both sides and the top of the body cover have to be sewn except the neck opening (*a*). The shoulders have to be established by sewing diagonal seams as indicated by the dotted lines in Fig. 1. The bottom of the rectangle remains open.

Fig. 5 gives the pattern for the legs. The middle axis (*a*) will have a length of 8 inches. The upper border should be $1\frac{3}{4}$ inches wide, the foot piece (*c*) $1\frac{1}{8}$ inches wide. The foot has to be pulled up a little with a few stitches as you did with the doll made of stockings (pages 18 and 19).

In Fig. 6, the arms are shown enlarged with the help of the graph pattern. The pattern for the arms will be approximately $1\frac{1}{2}$ inches wide.

After the cover of the body has been sewn, the stuffed legs are pulled through the body (Fig. 7) by starting from the bottom (arrow *a*) and emerging at the neck opening (*b-b*). The legs have to be pinned on and then sewn. Now, reverse the cover to its right side. Since the hole of the throat is very small it may take some patience to reverse the body cover, but once this is done, you can stuff the body, then sew the stuffed arms loosely on to the shoulders with hemming stitches.

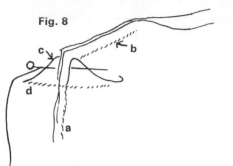

Fig. 8

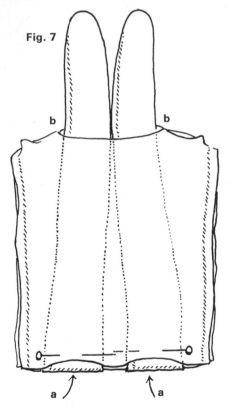

Fig. 7

In Fig. 8, *a* is the side seam, *b* is the diagonal seam, *c* is the crease of the material you folded, and *d* is the seam of the dart you sew across the material from one end of the fold to the other. Fig. 9 shows that you sew the arms on at the shoulder line.

After the body is stuffed and the limbs are sewn on, insert the semi-hard head with the throat ring and pull and sew the cloth tightly together above the ring.

An example of this doll is on page 76. Its face is painted with colored pencils. A wig

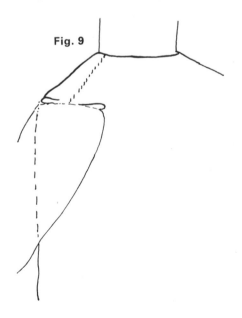

Fig. 9

To give the shoulder part a good-looking form, you should sew a dart before reversing and stuffing the body. To do this, make a fold across the side seam of the torso where it meets the diagonal seam inside the cloth.

Illus. 17. Dolls made from body-torso pattern are stuffed and provided with wigs.

was made from Icelandic lamb's wool. The size of the head without the wig is approximately $3\frac{1}{8}$ inches. The total size of the doll is 16 inches.

The so-called "Juten doll" is especially suitable to be fitted with a hard, movable head, as it is exceptionally stable. The paper pattern is shown in Fig. 1 to 3, page 82. The body size is 5 × 7 inches. The length of the pattern for the legs and feet is $11\frac{1}{2}$ inches. At the top border the legs are $2\frac{1}{2}$ inches wide, at the foot level 2 inches. The arm is shown on a graph pattern with which you can enlarge any part of the pattern. The arm's width

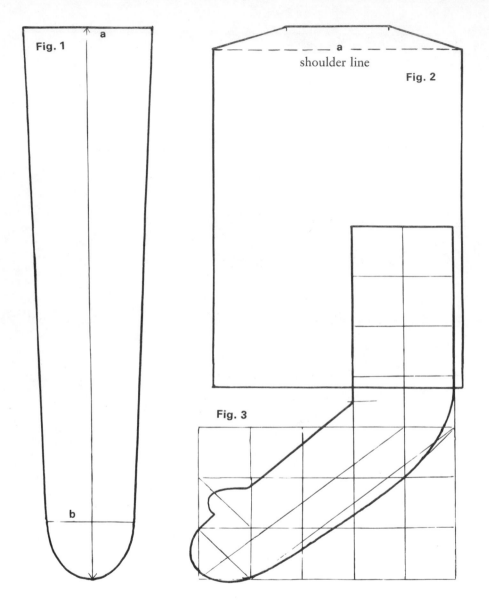

Fig. 1

a

b

Fig. 2

a

shoulder line

Fig. 3

should be approximately 1¾ inches. Sew the doll as described in the previous example. Hands are to be tied off.

The Juten doll figure on page 77 has a head modelled from sawdust material. The raw form was made water-tight with wax.

The face was painted with colored pencils. A wig from soft strings was sewn on to a skull cap in a spiral-like form. Size of the head is 3¾ inches. Size of the doll is 20¾ inches.

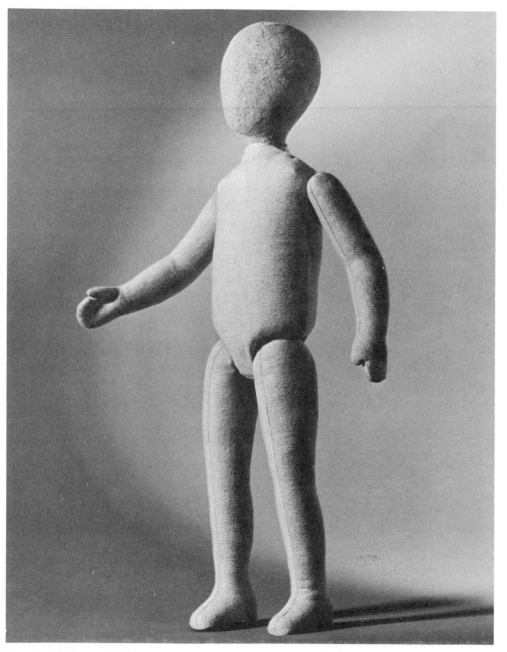

Illus. 18. This example shows that stuffed dolls can also be disc-jointed.

Stuffed Dolls with Disc Joints

Fig. 1   Fig. 3

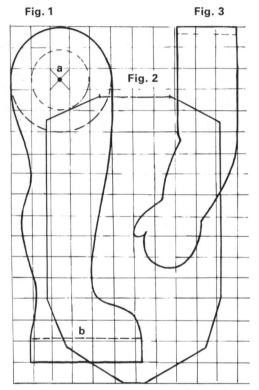

Fig. 2

The paper patterns to be cut for the body and limbs are given here above. Draw each pattern on a graph of squares with each square $\frac{1}{2}$ inch wide. For the covers you can use a mattress material like ticking or denim. At the top of the legs (Fig. 1) you have to mark the axis of the hips (a). At the feet a line (b) has to be drawn, as shown, on both pieces of your material. When sewing together these covers, you have to leave the top open at the neck, on each leg and on each

arm for stuffing later. To avoid too much spreading of the legs when the doll is put in a standing position, the inner part of the cover (see drawing on page 87) has to be cut $\frac{1}{8}$ of an inch higher (b). The bottom of each foot is also unsewn for now.

When the covers are sewn, you are ready to make and insert the joints, but we advise you to first reread the instructions on page 64 before going on with this doll.

Fig. 1 to 5, page 85, show how the hip spool is to be made.

Fig. 1: A strip of corrugated paper (a), $1\frac{1}{2}$ inches wide and 16 inches long, has to be covered with model material on the grooved side. This material has to be pressed into the grooves with a spatula or a knife (b).

Fig. 2: The strip then has to be wrapped around a pencil.

Fig. 3: Take the end of the roll (a) and fasten it to the roll with glue. Pin the end until the glue dries. Cover the flat ends (b) of the paper roll with model material and pull out the pencil. Final size of the roll, which has to be dried well, will be approximately $1\frac{1}{4}$ inches long and $1\frac{1}{2}$ inches in diameter.

Fig. 4: After the roll is smoothed with sandpaper, you draw the lines for the cuts (a and b), which you have to make diagonally as shown.

Fig. 5: With a fine saw, and if possible holding the roll in a vise, cut the roll into three parts as shown. The part to be inserted into the body should have a width of $1\frac{3}{8}$ inches at the top (a) and about $\frac{1}{2}$ inch at the bottom (b).

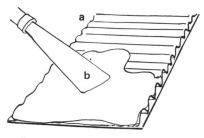

Fig. 1

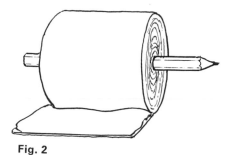

Fig. 2

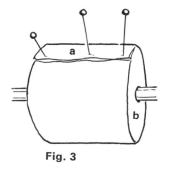

Fig. 3

Fig. 4

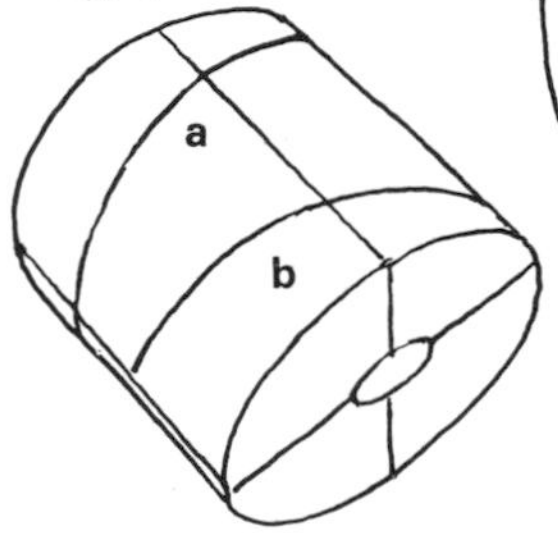

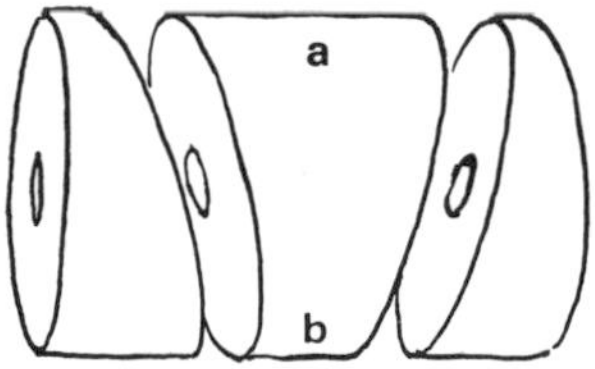

Fig. 5

Fig. 6

Fig. 7

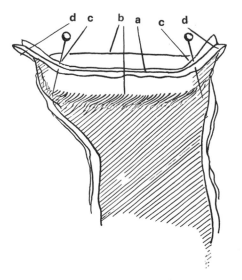

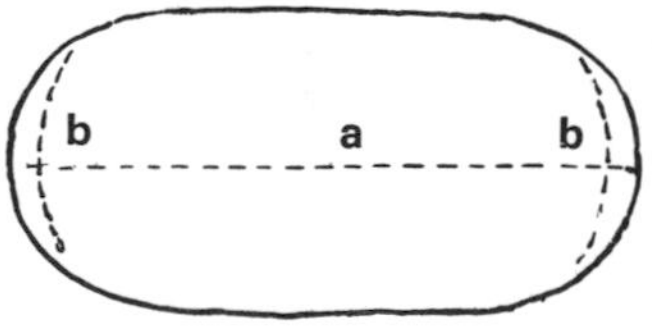

Fig. 6, at left: To make the sole of the foot, take the sewn leg cover, leave it inside-out, and fold the pattern material on both sides at *b*. The edges of the folds have to be made into a seam (*a*), which has to be spread flat. Two cross seams, each an inch long, have to be pinned and sewn (*c*). Leftover flaps (*d*) can be removed with a pair of scissors after sewing. Turn the foot-and-leg cover right side out.

Fig. 7: The sole of the foot seen from the bottom. The dotted line *a* represents the seam in the middle; the lines *b* are the cross seams.

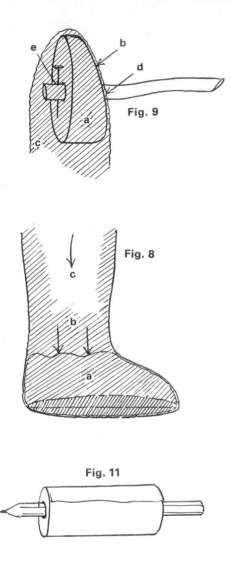

Fig. 9

Fig. 8

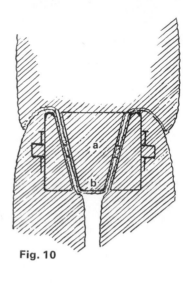

Fig. 10

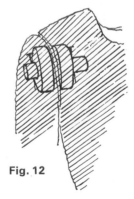

Fig. 12

Fig. 11

Fig. 8: To be sure that the doll stands properly, you have to put its center of gravity into the feet. The best filling material for this will be fine sand (*a*) which you should mix with glue so that it is slightly moistened. The legs and feet have to be in a standing position while being filled (*b*) with sand. After this is done, you stuff the remainder of the leg up to the thigh with cotton (*c*), and put it away for drying. Do this with both legs.

Fig. 9, above: The hip joint of the leg has to be inserted as shown in the diagram. First punch a small hole through the inner leg cover (*b*) at the axis. Pull thick rubber tubing (*d*) through that hole and through the hole of one leg-joint piece (*a*). Hold the tubing with a pin or nail (*e*). Then that leg can be completely stuffed. Pull the covering material of the leg well towards you at the top and sew it firmly into place.

Fig. 10: Both legs are now attached to the end of the body (*a*). Insert the middle portion of your paper roll (see Fig. 5) at the bottom of the body cover. Glue the roll into place if necessary. Punch small holes through the body cover material at the axis holes. Draw the rubber tubing from the finished leg through the body and anchor it with a pin or nail at the end of the hip joint inserted in the second leg. Finish the second leg by completing the stuffing and sewing as you did for the first leg.

To keep the leg well connected with the rubber tubing, it is advisable for two persons to work together on this part. One has to hold the doll; the other has to fasten the rubber tightly into position.

Fig. 11 and 12: If you wish joints for the arms of your doll, you have to apply some glue to a strip of wrapping paper which is 2 inches wide. Roll this strip around a pencil until it reaches a ¾-inch thickness. Let the roll dry, and then take a saw and divide the roll into four equal parts, which are attached at the shoulders with the help of

rubber tubing as shown. Follow the same steps for stuffing and attaching the arms as you did for the legs. The hands have to be stuffed like the feet and moderately flattened. If you use sawdust instead of sand for filling, the arms will not be too heavy. Finally, you stuff the body with cotton and insert the head, either movable or unmovable, hard or semi-hard.

Models of stuffed, jointed dolls are shown on pages 4, 83, 88 and the book cover. All of these dolls have movable, hard heads. Moistened colored pencils covered with a colorless nail polish were used to paint facial features. The model on page 4 has a wig made from nylon fibre, as described on page 54, Fig. 7.

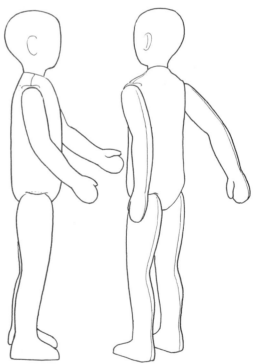

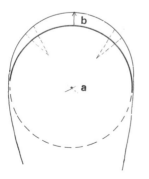

Inner leg cover has to be cut higher.

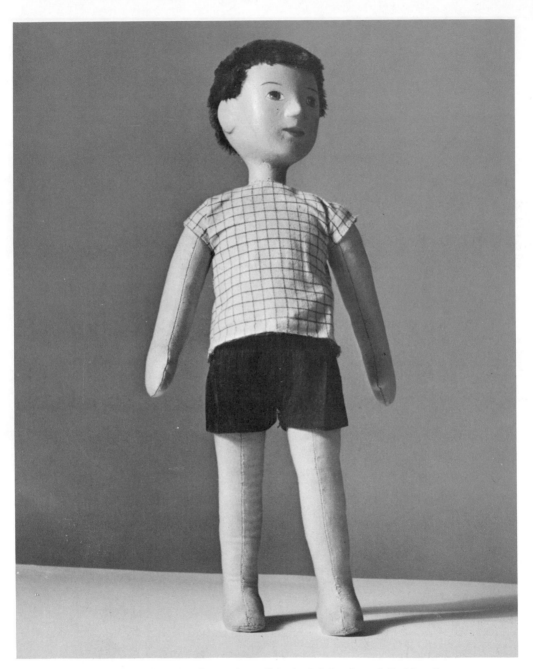

Illus. 19. Stuffed disc-jointed dolls are best fitted with hard modelled heads.

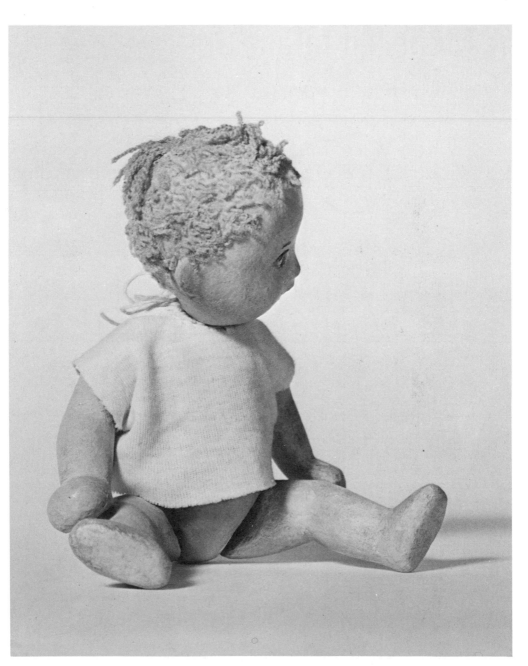

Illus. 20. Hard modelled, jointed dolls in infant form require different proportions.

A Modelled Infant Doll

The doll we describe here takes the form of a year-old baby. The proportions of a doll baby are different from those of other dolls. Here are the proportions as illustrated above: head 3/12, body 5/12, arms and legs 4/12 the size of the body. If you make the body of the doll baby short, the legs will look more natural. Also the baby's body will appear more natural to you when putting the doll baby into a sitting position.

Another typical characteristic of a baby's body is a short throat, which almost cannot be seen when the doll is sitting. A baby's neck is thin and keeps the head erect only with difficulty. Therefore, your doll's head may be tottering. A baby has: a large head with a very short face and a sparse growth of hair; a strongly bowed belly; a flat back, with the legs pulled towards the body, bent at the knees. The legs are thin and have almost the same thickness at the top as at the bottom. The foot is short and small. The arms are slender and also bent at the elbows. The hands are kept closed.

Each of the body parts will be modelled separately and then united at the joints.

Fig. 1: Two cardboard cut-outs of the head (a) have to be made.

Fig. 2: They are then glued together with model material over a rod (b). After this is done, the head is shaped from model material.

Fig. 3: Cut out two cardboard pieces for the body.

Fig. 4: Thick rubber tubing (c) will be used to make the head movable. This is to be glued between the cardboard framework for the body.

Fig. 5: The cardboard frames for the torso are then covered with model material. Small pieces of dowel are used to form hip and shoulder axes; these are later replaced with thick rubber tubing.

Fig. 6: Cut out the cardboard framework for the legs, which are then modelled (Fig. 7) as described in the chapter on shaping legs and arms. Fig. 8 and 9: Cut out and model the arms.

Fig. 10: After all six single parts have their final form, they are put together with rubber tubing as described in the chapter on modelled dolls with joints.

In the model on page 89, the body was painted in a light skin tone. Facial details were worked out with water-based paint, then rubbed glossy with a rag. The hair was made from wool yarn cut into small pieces and then glued directly on to the head. The size of the doll is 8½ inches, made from a graph pattern of 1-inch squares.

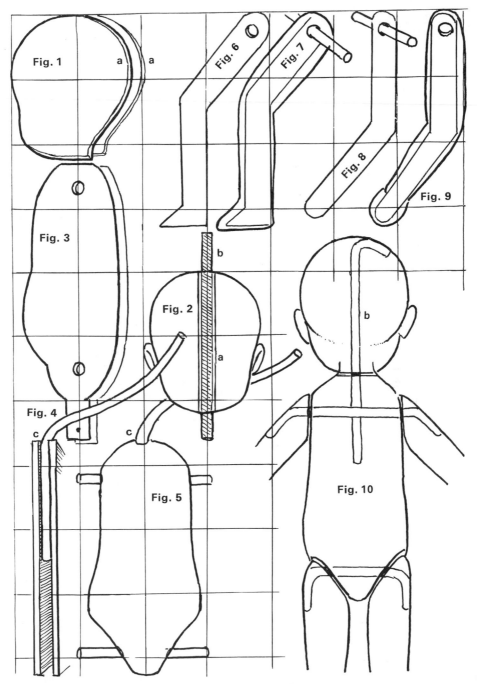

Fig. 1 a a

Fig. 6

Fig. 7

Fig. 8

Fig. 9

Fig. 3

b

Fig. 2

a

b

Fig. 4

c

c

Fig. 5

Fig. 10

91

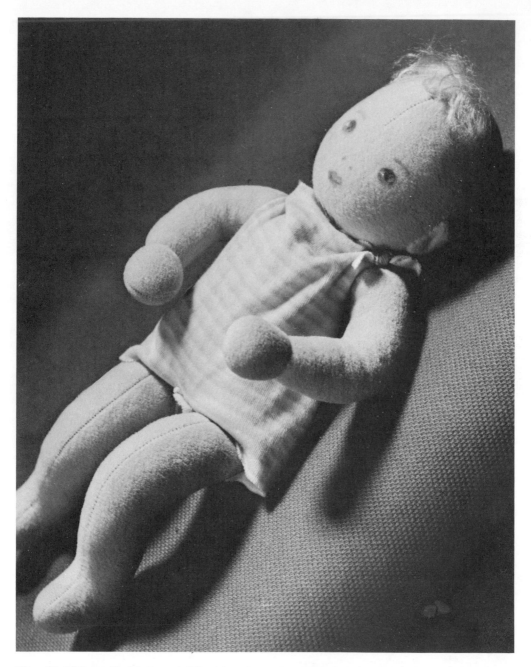

Illus. 21. This stuffed infant doll is made from the pattern on next page.

An Infant Doll of Stuffed Parts

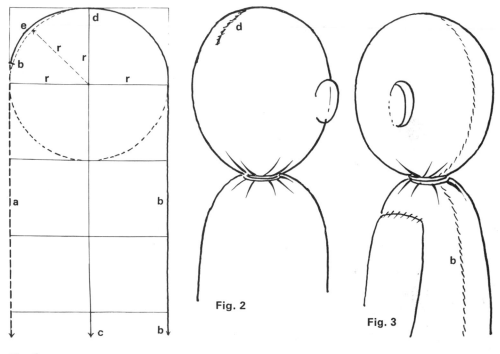

Fig. 1

Fig. 2

Fig. 3

The paper pattern here, above (Fig. 1) allows you to form the sparsely-haired scalp without any folds. The upper part of this pattern is used for the head; the lower part is used for shaping the body.

Place line *a* on the fold of your material. Cut along the line *b*, which includes the semi-circle and which will be the seam from the middle of the back across the middle line of the head to the onset of the hair in the front. Line *d-c* is the middle axis of the pattern. Each side of the squares on the pattern—and each of the radii (*r*)—represents 2 inches.

Line *d-c* should be about 11 inches. Note the deviation (*e*) of the paper pattern from the exact circle line. When cutting out the material do not forget to include an additional piece around the outline of the pattern for the seam. Patterns for arms and legs are given in Fig. 4, page 94. Each square represents 1 square inch.

When the head and body are made from one piece of material, Fig. 2 shows where the seam ends at the middle of the stuffed forehead (*d*); in Fig. 3, the back view, you see the seam going over the middle of the head. The

93

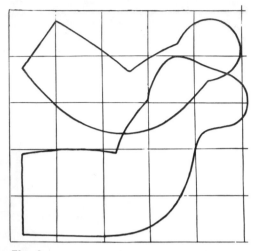

Fig. 4

throat is wrapped slightly above the middle of the stuffed cloth cylinder, so that the body and head are in proper proportion for an infant doll. The head is now sitting loosely as is desired for a doll baby. The arms and legs are made and attached in the usual manner.

A model of this doll is on page 92. The cover is a light, velvet material. The face is painted on with moistened colored pencils. A white dot in the eyes gives a natural expression. The hairs are made from fine embroidery yarn. The ears are attached separately to the doll.

You can also make the head and torso separately. In that case the head will get two covers. Fig. 1, right: The first cover is made from two pieces of your material, each 4 inches wide and 6½ inches long, plus margins for seams. Sew the cut material into a tube. Pull this tube together at the top, sew, turn inside out, and stuff. Then, wind the throat as described for Fig. 2, page 93.

Fig. 2: The face is separated from the scalp by a string which is glued and held with pins until the glue dries. The nose is put on as described on page 74.

To finish the head, you now have to take the second cover, made from the top part of the pattern on page 93, and pull it over the head. Length of the line *d-c* will be 6½ inches; width of the pattern will be 4 inches.

Fig. 1 to 4, page 95, shows exactly how the second cover gets pulled over the head. The folds are pulled to the back (Fig. 2) and kept there with pins (Fig. 3). These folds are sewn by placing the seam across the neck as shown by line *a* on Fig. 4. After sewing this cross seam and tying off the throat, you can put on the ears, which will cover the beginning of the cross seam on both sides.

For the body, sew two pieces of material 6½ × 4 inches, plus seam allowances. Leave a hole at the top of the tubelike cover for stuffing the doll. This hole can be sewn together after stuffing, but still a small opening must remain into which the head will be pushed and therein sewn.

Whether you make a soft, infant doll like this one, or a hard-modelled, fully-jointed doll—or any other kind described in this book—you will experience the pleasure of creating an artful object. There are no limits to the variety of dolls you can fashion. Using the guide lines in this book and your own

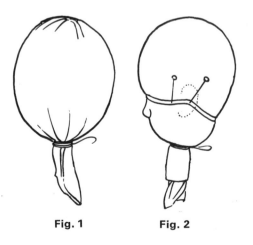

Fig. 1   **Fig. 2**

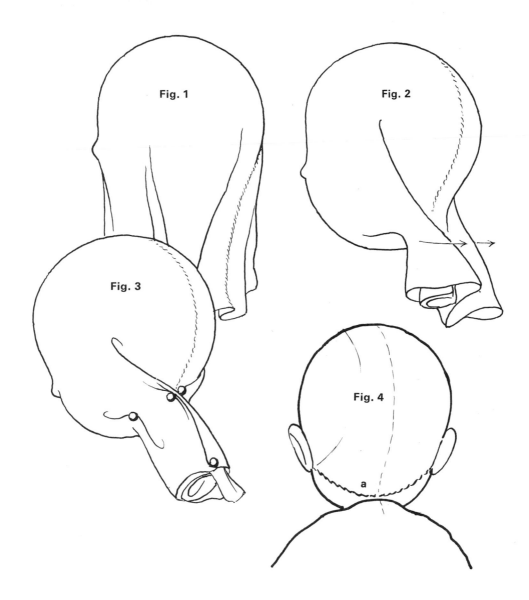

Fig. 1

Fig. 2

Fig. 3

Fig. 4

a

taste and imagination, you can experiment with all the techniques used here and, perhaps, come up with new ones. Making dolls is a craft that will enrich you and bring results that will be treasured for their uniqueness.

Index